Teachers' Resource Book

SCAFFOLDS

Written by
Dennis Watts

HOPSCOTCH
EDUCATIONAL PUBLISHING

Published by Hopscotch
A division of MA Education Ltd
St Jude's Church, Dulwich Road
Herne Hill, London SE24 0PB
Tel: 020 7738 5454

© 2007 MA Education Ltd

Written by Dennis Watts
Series design by Blade Communications
Cover illustration by Kirsty Wilson
Illustrated by Jane Bottomley
Printed in the UK by CLE, St Ives, Huntingdon,
Cambridgeshire

ISBN 1-904307-33-7
ISBN 978-1-904307-33-4

Dennis Watts hereby asserts his moral right to be
identified as the author of this work in accordance
with the Copyright, Designs and Patents Act, 1988.

Year 3

Non-fiction writing
SCAFFOLDS

CONTENTS

INTRODUCTION

Non-fiction Writing Scaffolds Year 3 is intended for use in schools to help teach children how to write effectively in a variety of non-fiction genres. It improves children's ability to organise their writing so that it has purpose by familiarising them with a system of planning which they can apply to any title. As they work through the units, the children assemble a portfolio of non-fiction texts containing genre-specific vocabulary and writing features. The chosen text types coincide with those in the Literacy Framework's text-level objectives.

Many non-fiction texts are essentially cross-curricular. Thus the ability to write specifically and purposefully about a subject will benefit other areas of study.

Each unit includes information and activities on at least one sentence-level objective. Therefore the book also enhances the children's knowledge of grammar, punctuation and style.

THE PROGRAMME CONTAINS:

a teachers' book comprising:

- notes for teachers on the genres
- a bibliography for each genre
- copies of exemplar texts together with teaching notes
- guidance on how to develop grammar and punctuation skills in children's writing
- guidance on how to write in the particular genre and on specific features of each non-fiction text.

a resource book of photocopiable material comprising:

- illustrated versions of the exemplar texts especially produced for children
- notes for the children on understanding the grammar and punctuation (optional reference material)
- photocopiable activity sheets to reinforce the grammar and punctuation (optional)
- notes and tips for the children on writing non-fiction texts (optional reference material)
- differentiated scaffolds which give the children choices and guide them through the course of the text they are about to write
- vocabulary banks for them to use and add to.

HOW TO USE THE PROGRAMME

1 After examining texts in the target genre, read and discuss the exemplar text with the children, using the notes in the margin to highlight the examples of the unit's teaching point and writing feature. The children should follow the text using their own illustrated version from the resource book.

2 Next, read through and explain the 'Understanding the grammar and punctuation' section of the unit. The children can do the activities together, either orally or using whiteboards, or independently on paper.

3 Then explain the 'Helpful hints' and 'Writing features' sections of the unit to the children.

4 Read through the scaffolds with the children. Then give them the differentiated word banks and ask them to record their own vocabulary suggestions in the space provided.

5 Give the children time to plan, write and edit their non-fiction text. Each child can then store the best copies in a writing folder.

NOTES

When using the scaffolds, give the children strict time limits to plan and write each of the sections. This will give them practice in writing timed non-fiction texts as preparation for the Key Stage 2 writing test.

However, the system is entirely flexible. The activities in each unit, from reading the exemplar to composing their own text using the scaffolds, can be used in shared or guided time, with the children working collaboratively or individually.

The order of activities for each unit corresponds exactly with the sequence for the teaching of writing outlined in Grammar for Writing (DfEE 0107/200). First the model can be discussed and its grammatical and thematic features interrogated during shared reading. Next the grammar and punctuation activities can be undertaken to reinforce the children's understanding of the relevant sentence-level objectives. The helpful hints section, scaffolds, and vocabulary banks support the teacher and children in shared writing sessions and in subsequent guided and independent writing.

The method works well with children of all abilities and with bilingual pupils, as it offers the security of a detailed framework and a bank of appropriate vocabulary together with the challenge of a grammar and writing features component for each unit.

The units fulfil the text-level and sentence-level requirements of the NLS Framework for Year 3 and revise components from Year 2. The units may be used specifically in literacy lessons or they may be linked with work in other curriculum areas and used accordingly.

TERM 1
UNIT 1

Genre: reports – information texts (T21; T22)
Grammar: verbs and verb tenses (S3; S4)
Punctuation: revision of capital letters and full stops (S11; S12)
Writing feature: organising and presenting ideas, labelled diagrams (T21; T22)

UNIT 2

Genre: reports – holiday guides (T22)
Grammar: verbs; verb tenses (S3; S4) use of third person
Punctuation: devices for presenting text (S9)
Writing features: headlines, presentation, content, language and layout (T21; T22)

UNIT 3

Genre: instructions – making or doing something
Grammar: verbs, especially second person verbs for instructional writing (S10) adjectives for clarity (not effect) (S2)
Punctuation: commas for lists (S6; S7)
Writing features: how instructions are organised – numbering, lists (T14; T16)

TERM 2
UNIT 4

Genre: instructions – directions
Grammar: plurals (S4)
Punctuation: use of capitalisation (S8)
Writing features: the importance of sequencing and diagrams (T16; T21)

UNIT 5

Genre: note taking – historical information
Grammar: deleting words and retaining meaning (S9)
Punctuation: commas (S6; S7)
Writing: how to make notes, identifying key words, using simple formats for notes, using shortened forms of words (T17; T20; T25; T26)

UNIT 6

Genre: recounts – informal letters
Grammar: pronouns (S2)
Punctuation: letter punctuation (S12; S8)
Writing features: features of personal letters, email messages, style and vocabulary appropriate to reader (T20)

TERM 3
UNIT 7

Genre: recounts – formal letters
Grammar: grammatical agreement of pronouns and verbs (S3)
Punctuation: organising letters into paragraphs (S23)
Writing features: features of formal letters selecting appropriate style and vocabulary (T20)

UNIT 8

Genre: recounts – newspaper reports
Grammar: adjectives to get attention and interest (S2), verbs – past tense (S4)
Punctuation: dialogue punctuation (S4)
Writing features: features of newspaper reports (T22, T21)

UNIT 9

Genre: explanations: encyclopaedias
Grammar: joining complex sentences using a wide range of conjunctions (S5)
Punctuation: commas and dashes (S7)
Writing features: features of encyclopaedia texts (T17; T24)

Pet Pygmy Goats

General Information

Pygmy goats originally came from parts of Africa – in particular from Nigeria and Cameroon. They are not completely white like many goats that are kept to produce milk. They can be brown, white with black or brown markings or many shades of grey and sometimes with a shade of blue. Some of the best looking pygmy goats have an attractive combination of several of these colours.

These goats are very small: most are less than 60 centimetres from the ground to the top of the back of the goat. Most have a barrel-shaped body with a fat stomach and quite short legs. They grow horns as they grow older although sometimes the horns are removed to make them safer as pets. A beard usually grows under the chin. There are also two small tassels called 'toggles' on the neck. A short tail is usually held up, looking rather like a flag! Females have udders that produce milk for baby goats, which are called 'kids'.

Some pygmy goats were taken from Africa to zoos in Britain, often to be kept in paddocks where children can stroke them. Their kids were often sold as pets. Pygmy goats make great pets. In some ways, these small goats are similar to dogs. Goats enjoy human company, and will sit as close to a human as possible. They are very playful, frequently butting balls and running around. They also like to butt each other playfully.

Parts of a pygmy goat

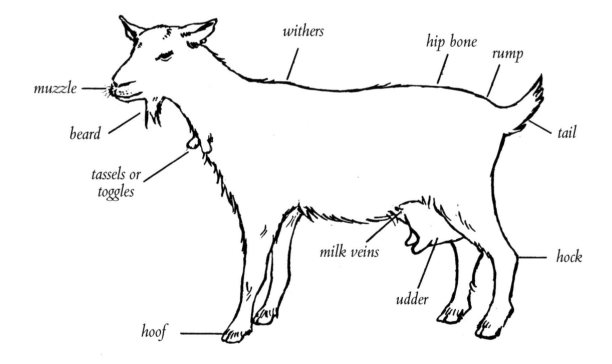

withers
hip bone
rump
muzzle
beard
tassels or toggles
tail
milk veins
hock
udder
hoof

Food

Goat Feed and supplements

Goats do **not** eat everything they can find! They may sniff and nibble at things, like clothes, but they certainly do not eat them! In fact pygmy goats can be quite fussy; for example, if a piece of dirt such as mud gets on their food, they will not eat it because it is dirty!

Pet pygmy goats should be fed plenty of hay and a special goat mix which can be bought from shops that supply farmers. They also enjoy most vegetables that are eaten by humans. It is best to give small amounts of various types of leftover vegetables, such as carrots, along with plenty of hay. Eating too much of one type of food can cause bloat – a painfully swollen stomach. The goats love to eat treats such as the occasional biscuit but remember they are vegetarians!

Their food can be put in a bowl of the type used for feeding a large dog. It is best to put hay in a rack to keep it off the floor of the goat shed where it could get dirty. It is important to provide a mineral lick, which is a brick-sized solid lump of salt and other minerals, which the goats will enjoy licking. This helps to keeps them healthy. Two or more water bowls (about the size of a washing up bowl) should be kept full and clean. They should be checked at least once a day and more often in hot weather. Smaller water containers are not a good idea because the goats will pick them up with their mouths, play with them and butt them!

They can be fed the goat mix once a day or it can be divided into two portions so they get it twice a day. They will soon get used to being fed at a particular time and will bleat if you are late!

Goats will search for food to eat in their paddock, such as grass and leaves from trees. They browse rather than graze. This means they bite off the best bits while walking around, rather than steadily eating grass like grazing sheep. Pygmy goats will eat garden flowers, particularly roses, which can get them into trouble if they are not kept away from them! It is important to read about poisonous plants, perhaps in books in the library, to make sure you can recognise them and make sure goats do not eat them.

Shelter

Pygmy goats need a place to sleep in at night and a paddock – an area of grass – to eat and move about on during the day. A simple shed will do for their night shelter and this is where their hay, water and other food should be put. They do not need a large field. An area large enough for them to run around and get exercise is sufficient.

Pygmy goats are experts at escaping! They think this is great fun. It is not because they want to run away but because they are curious and want to explore ... and eat the roses! It is important to have a strong fence all round their paddock with a gate fastened with two bolts. They are clever animals and soon learn how to undo a bolt so they should be fitted where the goats cannot reach them. Thick wooden posts and rails are necessary; one and a half metres high. (They can jump high off the ground when feeling lively!) Strong wire netting called 'sheep wire' must be fixed to the wooden fence to keep them in. Pygmy goats do not like being tethered (tied up using collar and lead) unless it is for only about fifteen minutes at a time and there is plenty of interesting food to eat!

They should have boxes and benches to sit and play on plus some balls they will like to butt around!

Goats also like each other's company. A pygmy goat must never be kept on its own. They are herd animals and one goat would be lonely and unhappy.

Health and care

Pygmy goats need their hooves trimmed regularly; otherwise they will start skidding everywhere! To do this you need to tether the goat to a fence and give it some greenery to eat to take its mind off what is going on at the hoof-end of its body. Hoof trimming is like cutting toenails and does them no harm.

Pygmy goats will grow horns. Some goat keepers leave them to grow, but a horned goat, as a pet, can accidentally cause damage to people, fences and other goats. Many pygmy goats have their horn 'buds' removed by a vet when they are very young and before they start to grow horns. It is much more difficult for a vet to remove horns after they have grown.

In autumn the pygmy goat grows a thick fur coat and a layer of wool next to its skin. This keeps it warm enough not to need heating in its shed. After the winter the goat's coat moults, as the weather gets warmer. This makes it look very 'shaggy' and untidy for a time. It may be necessary to give the goat a shampoo to wash away the old coat and clean the skin. It is best and kinder to do this on a warm day. The goat should be tethered and fed with leaves to take its mind off the washing as it will not like it. It should be sprayed with a hose and a special animal shampoo used to get rid of any dandruff and loose hair. The shampoo should be rinsed off and the goat thoroughly dried with some old towels, trying not to let it chew the towels!

Pygmy goats are usually very healthy. They are normally lively, happy, bright eyed, frequently bleating, keen to feed, friendly to humans and, most of the time, their tails are held up higher than their backs, showing they are happy. (Except, of course, when feeling sleepy!) If a goat is not like this, it is important a vet is called to see it.

Your vet will advise on any forms to be completed for a government department, simple regular treatments to prevent worms in the stomach and annual vaccinations that are important to prevent some illnesses.

The above text is based on the website www.henryandjoey.com about two pet pygmy goats by David Watts at the age of 12 in 1999.

Understanding the grammar and punctuation

Verbs
Verbs are doing or being words.
They tell you what a person or thing is doing.

All sentences have verbs.

In autumn the pygmy goat <u>grows</u> a thick fur coat.

Goats <u>enjoy</u> human company, and <u>will sit</u> as close to a human as possible.

Verb tenses
The tense of a verb can be
past, present or future.

They <u>think</u> escaping <u>is</u> great fun. (present)

The pygmy goat breed <u>was</u> orginally <u>found</u> in Africa. (past)

Your vet <u>will advise</u> on any forms to be completed ... (future)

Capital letters and full stops
Every sentence begins with a capital letter
and ends with a full stop.

Pygmy goats make great pets.

Pygmy goats are usually very healthy.

Verbs

Read the five sentences below. Underline all the verbs you can find and then put a cross beside any of the sentences that do not make sense because a verb is missing

1. When we go on holiday we put our dog in kennels. _____

2. Our pet goat after by neighbours. _____

3. Some farmers accommodation for goats. _____

4. We all went to a zoo last Saturday. _____

5. Animals food every day. _____

Read through the following sentences carefully. Then rewrite each one using the correct tense of the verb.

1. We will go/went to the cinema tomorrow.

   _____

2. I see/saw him yesterday.

   _____

3. Tim catch/caught a pike last week.

   _____

4. Helen run/ran after her sister who had forgotten her bag.

   _____

5. She ate/eat all of the cake this morning.

   _____

On the back of this sheet, write four sentences about pygmy goats using the verbs below.

escape   eat   play   grow

Capital letters and full stops

Read through the paragraph below.
Then put in all the capital letters and full stops.
You should end up with six sentences.

Milking goats

goats are often kept because they provide milk female pygmy goats can

provide a small amount of milk but it is difficult to milk their small udders

the larger breeds of goat provide much more milk mr thomas, who lives near

brighton, has a herd of goats providing milk that is sold in the supermarket

he delivers the milk every monday, wednesday and friday some people are

allergic to cow's milk but can drink milk from goats without problems

Find some more information about goats. You might like to find out about the different breeds of goats or how they live in the wild, for example.

Write your information here. Remember to use capital letters and full stops.

_____

_____

_____

_____

_____

_____

_____

Helpful hints for writing information

✦ Plan what you will write so that it is easy to read. Make sure it is organised in a sensible order so that it is easy to understand.

✦ When you have planned, you will be ready to start writing the information. Use a bold title to make it clear what the information is about.

✦ Start with an introduction that includes general information and gives some important facts.

✦ Try to include interesting points and even amusing information if you can. This will help to get the reader interested.

✦ Organise the information by setting it out with clear headings and subheadings where this helps the reader to find pieces of information.

✦ Use the third person when you write. This means:

Do not write using the words: 'I', 'me', 'myself', 'mine', 'we', 'us', 'ourselves' or 'our'.

Do use: 'he', 'she', 'it', 'him', 'her', 'they' and 'their'.

Goats do not eat everything they can find! They may sniff and nibble at things, like clothes, but they certainly do not eat them.

✦ Use clear, simple language. Keep most of your sentences short. Try not to use words that the reader may not know, unless you make it clear what

the word means with a short explanation.

✦ Include drawings or diagrams to make parts of the information clear. These must have a title and plenty of clear labels.

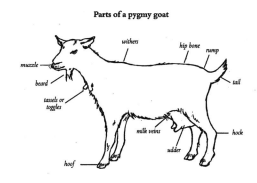

Parts of a pygmy goat

A diagram without any writing on it does not give much information and will only decorate the page. Photographs can be included. A computer can be used to place photographs and labels in the right place.

✦ Make sure that you only write about what is in the title and headings. Don't write about other things.

✦ Make sure you do not repeat things in your explanation unless it is to emphasise a very important point.

✦ The length of the information will depend on what you are writing about but try not to make it so long that the reader gets bored.

Information writing
Scaffold 1

You are going to write some information about an animal.
To help you plan your report, use the framework below.
Choose one option from each stage.

Stage One

Choose one of the following:

a) A pet animal you know a lot about.
b) A zoo animal.
c) A farm animal.

Write the name of the animal as a heading at the top of your page.

Remember: write about what you already know and find out extra information from books, the Internet, CD-Roms and from people who know about the type of animal you have chosen.

Stage Two

Write the subheading: General information

Use your first paragraphs to write some interesting, perhaps amusing, information about the animal to get the reader's interest.

Choose from the following:

a) Describe the animal. Say what it looks like.

b) Say where it comes from in the world.

c) Say whether there are different types, colours and so on.

d) Say why it makes a good pet/needs to be kept in a zoo/why it is used on farms.

e) Draw and label a diagram of the animal.

Stage Three

Write the subheading: Food
Write some paragraphs about what the animal eats and its feeding habits.
Choose from the following:

a) Say what the animal usually eats and drinks. How often?

b) Describe any special tips about preparing the food.

c) Describe the best types of food and water containers to use.

d) Say what special things need to be remembered about feeding.

Stage Four

Write the subheading: Shelter
Write some paragraphs about what the animal needs as a home.
Choose from the following:

a) Write about what the animal usually does during the day and
   the night.

b) Say what kind of shelter and bedding it needs and how to
   clean/look after the bedding.

c) Say what special things need to be remembered to keep the
   animal safe.

d) Say whether it needs a different kind of shelter in the
   summer than in the winter. Say why.

WHICH SHALL
I WRITE ABOUT?

Stage Five

Write the subheading: Health and care
Write some paragraphs about how to look after the animal so that it
stays healthy. Choose from the following:

a) Explain what needs to be done to keep the animal healthy.
   Does it need regular bathing/brushing/trimming?
   Explain how this is done correctly.

b) Say if it needs regular medicines or pills to keep it healthy,
   for example worming tablets.

c) Write about vet visits and why these might be necessary.

d) Say how to keep the animal and its shelter clean.

Information writing
Vocabulary Bank 1

animal	elephant	male
appearance		meat
aviary	farm	milking
	feeding	
barn	female	paddock
basket	fencing	parrot
bedding		
bird seed	gerbil	rabbit
bowl	giraffe	
bucket	grooming	shed/shelter
budgerigar	guinea-pig	sheep
bull		size
	hamster	straw
cage	hay	
care	horse	tinned food
coloured	housing	
		vaccination
dangerous	lion	
disease	llama	water

My own words

Information writing
Scaffold 2

You are going to write some information on a sea creature.
To help you plan your report, use the framework below.
Choose one option from each stage, or use your own ideas.

Stage One

Choose one of the following:

a) A type of sea fish.

b) A sea creature other than a fish; for example, a crab, squid or seal.

Use what you already know and find out more from books, the Internet, CD-Roms and so on.

Stage Two

Write the subheading: General information
Write some interesting facts in your first paragraph to get the reader's attention.
Choose from the following:

a) Describe the creature. Include its usual length, width, shape, colours and general appearance.

b) Draw and label a diagram of the creature to show the different body parts.

c) Write about the creature's life-cycle. Describe how it changes as it grows from a baby into an adult. What is the average adult weight?

d) Say how the creature defends itself from attack from other creatures. Is it harmful/useful to humans?

Stage Three

Write the subheading: Habitat
Write some paragraphs about where the creature lives.
Include details of anything that you might call its home.
Choose from the following:

a) Describe where the creature usually lives – does it prefer shallow waters or ocean depths? Where in the world is it found?

b) Describe how the creature lives in its habitat – does it stay in one main area, does it migrate to different places at different times of the year?

c) Find out about any dangers to the creature's habitat. Is pollution or over-fishing a problem, for example?

Stage Four

Write the subheading: Food
Write some paragraphs about what the creature eats and its feeding habits. Choose from the following:

a) Describe what the creature usually eats and how it gets its food.

b) Describe any special body parts that the creature uses for capturing or eating its food.

c) Say where the creature hunts for its food. Does it do this at special times of the day? What does it look out for?

Stage Five

Write the subheading: Relationship with humans
Write some paragraphs about how the creature helps or is used by humans. Choose from the following:

a) Find out if your creature is eaten or used by humans in some way. How is it caught/ prepared/used? Is the creature fished/used for scientific purposes/studied in some way?

I NEED TO FIND OUT IF ANY HUMANS EAT IT.

b) Say how humans have had an effect on this creature. Have humans helped or hurt the creature? Has the creature helped or hurt humans? What might the future hold?

Information writing
Vocabulary bank 2

beach	gills	scavenger
		sea-bed
coast	habitat	seal
cod	haddock	shark
conger eel	hermit crab	shell
crab		shellfish
current	jellyfish	shrimp
	lobster	squid
dangerous		sting
defence	ocean	
		tail
environment	penguin	temperature
escape	pincers	tide
estuary	plaice	trawler
	pollution	
fight	prawn	water
fin	predator	waves
flippers		whale
		wreck

My own words

A Guide to The South Hams Area of Devon

Location

The South Hams area is on the south coast of Devon, to the south of Dartmoor. It is between Plymouth and Torbay. The area includes a coastline with beautiful cliffs, sandy beaches and sheltered inlets. The beaches are some of the best in the country, often combining sand and rock pools with excellent scenery.

How to get there

The motorways M4 and M5 connect London with Devon and much of the midlands and north, via the M6. The A38 road continues from the M5 through Devon with turnings to the towns of South Hams.

Fast Intercity Express trains run to Devon from London and Birmingham many times a day.

They stop at Exeter and Newton Abbot. The fastest service takes just over two hours from London to Exeter (St Davids).

There are also flights to Exeter and Plymouth airports.

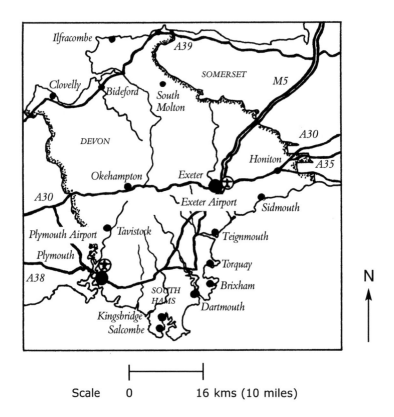

Scale   0   16 kms (10 miles)

Typical Monthly Temperatures and Sunshine Hours For South Hams, Devon		
Month	Usual daytime temperature	Hours of sunshine
January	8	52
February	8	67
March	10	110
April	13	153
May	16	185
June	19	189
July	21	192
August	21	172
September	19	134
October	15	89
November	11	70
December	9	49

Weather

This part of Britain has a good climate for holidays. The weather can change at any time, as in all of Britain, but the following are the usual features of the area's weather:

- plenty of sunshine in the summer;
- temperatures usually quite warm in summer;
- the average number of days with no rain is high in the summer;
- winter is mild compared with many other parts of the country.

The countryside

The countryside changes from the high, hilly moorland scenery to the north, to very green hills where cattle and sheep graze towards the south. In many places good views can be enjoyed over lush green farmland and out to the sea beyond. Ploughed fields have an unusual red colour because red sandstone colours the soil. Many country lanes are very narrow and run deep in cuttings worn into the sandstone by horse and carts before the roads were surfaced with tarmac. The towns and pretty villages have many interesting old buildings.

Places to visit include **Kingsbridge, Dartmouth, Totnes, Salcombe, Modbury, Hope Cove, Thurlestone** and **Torcross.**

An unusual trip by tractor

An example of an interesting trip is the drive south to the town of **Bigbury on Sea.** The road winds through very narrow deep cuttings and across lovely scenery to a beautiful beach near **Burgh Island.** This island is reached at high tide by going on *a tractor ride* across the beach and into the shallow sea at high tide. When the tractor drives out of the sea onto the island's beach, visitors can reach the hotel and old Pilchard Inn on the island.

Some Places to Visit

SALCOMBE

The town is a splendid sight in the summer. The green slopes of the South Hams hills make a background to the estuary full of white, tan and red sails. *Very attractive small, sheltered, sandy beaches nestle in rocky coves around the waterways.* These beaches are ideal for family days on the beach.

The Museum of Maritime and Local History at Custom Quay in Salcombe shows how the town grew on its important shipping and yachting activities.

Everyone can find something to enjoy. The town has beaches, coastal walking, boating, varied shops in tiny side streets and a variety of restaurants and public houses. Salcombe is one of the main yachting centres in England. Many visitors arrive by boat and in summer, there can be ten visitors for every local resident.

There are many hotels, guest houses and cottages to rent with *fascinating views of sea and scenery.* Some of the nearby caravan sites are *within easy reach of beaches.*

The Cookworthy Museum in the main street includes a reconstruction of an Edwardian chemist shop, a traditional farm and an outdoor gallery of farm equipment.

KINGSBRIDGE

Kingsbridge is a busy market town inland from Salcombe and at the inland end of the fascinating channels and inlets of the sea reached from Salcombe.

Kingsbridge has many different types of shops, a cinema, a sports centre, an indoor heated swimming pool, bowls rink and nightclub. In the 13th century the Abbot of Buckfast Abbey gave permission for his monks to start an open-air market on the quay to sell their fruit, vegetables, thick cream and honey. There are still regular *weekly markets* on the quay.

There are many footpaths and country lanes for walker and cyclist access to the countryside with stunning scenery. There are plenty of pubs and inns along the routes providing lunch stops. Restaurants provide cream teas on the lawn.

There are plenty of hotels and bed and breakfast farmhouses as well as cottages to rent for holidays. Campers and caravanners will find sites ranging from simple farm fields to touring parks with comprehensive facilities.

Attractions for all the family include outdoor adventure parks with fair and wet weather facilities, farm attractions, riding, swimming, sailing, sail-boarding, golf, tennis, cycling, National Trust properties, fishing, boat hire, and power-boating.

Excursions to other towns and cities

Larger towns and cities are less than an hour away from the South Hams area by car. **Plymouth** and **Exeter** have theatres, cinemas and historical attractions such as Exeter cathedral.

The South Hams has fascinating small towns such as Dartmouth and Totnes but a short distance from here are the much larger towns of **Paignton** and **Torquay** which provide an interesting contrast with all the holiday amusements and entertainments of big seaside resorts.

The South Hams area provides a huge range of opportunities to enjoy on a holiday. These range from walks in the countryside, meals in restaurants in pretty villages and quiet boating activities, to the fun of a beach holiday and the nearby facilities of large holiday resorts and cities.

Understanding the grammar and punctuation

Verbs

Verbs are doing or being words. They tell you what a person or thing is doing.

All sentences have verbs.

The motorways M4 and M5 <u>connect</u> London with Devon...

When the tractor <u>drives</u> out of the sea...

Verb tenses

When writing a report such as an information text or a holiday guide the verbs are written in the present tense.

The South Hams area <u>is</u> on the south coast of Devon.

The road <u>winds</u> through very narrow deep cuttings.

Ways of presenting information

There are many different ways that writing can be set out to make certain parts of the information stand out from the rest.

For example:

1. Headings in bold and capitals   **KINGSBRIDGE**

2. Subheadings in bold   **The countryside**

3. Words in italics   *tractor ride*

4. Inset text

> The Museum of Maritime and Local History at Custom Quay in Salcombe shows how the town grew on its important shipping and yachting activities.

Verbs

Look at the pictures below. Write a verb for each one for what is happening.

_____ _____ _____ _____

_____ _____ _____ _____

Read the sentences below. Choose a verb from the box to complete each one. Make sure the verb is in the present tense.

| provides/provided | swim/swam | included/include | was/is |
| drives/drove | sail/sailed | fly/flew | found/find |

1. The nearby city _____ good opportunities to go shopping.

2. Sailing _____ very enjoyable in the sheltered estuary.

3. Most hotels _____ breakfast in their daily rate.

4. The coach _____ through excellent scenery.

5. Many people _____ interesting shells on the beach.

6. You can _____ a kite on the big beach.

7. Older children _____ yachts on the calm water in the estuary.

8. Children _____ in the warm sea in summer.

Ways of presenting information

Complete the following as instructed.

1. *Circle the word in bold.*	Exeter	**Exeter**	Exeter
2. *Circle the word in italics.*	*fascinating*	fascinating	FASCINATING
3 *Circle the word in capital letters.*	map	MAP	**map**
4. *Circle the underlined word.*	<u>rainfall</u>	rainfall	*rainfall*

Circle the best lettering for a main heading in the examples below.

Holiday Guidebook

HOLIDAY GUIDEBOOK

HOLIDAY GUIDEBOOK

Holiday Guidebook

HOLIDAY GUIDEBOOK

Say why you chose this one.

_____

_____

Circle the sentence that you think is written to make it look very important.

The cliffs are dangerous.   *The cliffs are dangerous.*   **The cliffs are dangerous.**

Say why you chose this one.

_____

_____

On the back of this sheet, design a page for a guidebook for the area where you live.
Make sure you think carefully about how you will set it out.

Helpful hints for writing a holiday guide

✦ Find information about the area by reading guidebooks and talking to people who know about the subject. For example, tourist information officers and travel agents can be very helpful. Plan what you will write so it is easy to read. Make sure it is organised in a sensible order so that it is easy to understand.

✦ When you have finished your planning, you will be ready to start writing the information. Use a **bold** title to make clear what the information is about.

✦ Start with an introduction that will include general information giving some important facts. Try to include interesting and funny things to get the reader's attention.

✦ Use headings and subheadings. This helps the reader to find the information they want.

✦ Use the third person when you write. This means:

Do not write using the words: 'I', 'me', 'myself', 'mine', 'we', 'us', 'ourselves' or 'our'.

Do use: 'he', 'she', 'it', 'his', 'hers', 'they' and 'theirs'.

✦ Use clear, simple language. Keep most of your sentences short.

✦ Include drawings to make parts of the information clear. These must have a title and plenty of clear labels.

✦ A chart is a good way of showing figures. Be sure to give it a bold title and a heading on each column of the chart. For example:

Typical Monthly Temperatures and Sunshine Hours For South Hams, Devon		
Month	**Usual daytime temperature**	**Hours of sunshine**
January	8	52
February	8	67
March	10	110
April	13	153
May	16	185
June	19	189
July	21	192
August	21	172
September	19	134
October	15	89
November	11	70
December	9	49

✦ Make sure that what you write is only about what is in the title and headings. Don't write about other things.

✦ Make sure you do not repeat things.

✦ Try not to make it so long that the reader will get bored when reading it!

Holiday guide
Scaffold 1

You are going to write a guide to a holiday area.
To help you write your guide, use the framework below.
Choose one option from each stage.

Stage One

Choose one of the following types of holiday areas:

a) an island;
b) a mountain area;
c) a beach area.

Now choose a real holiday place in this type of area.

Write the name of the place in large, bold letters for your heading.
Then find out as much information you can about the place.

Use the library, the internet and CD-Roms to help you.

Stage Two

Write the subheading: Location
Choose from the following to write about:

WHICH SHALL
I CHOOSE?

a) Describe where the place is. What towns is it near?

b) Draw a map showing where it is. Label it.

c) Write about some of the main things to do there.

d) Say why people like to go there on holiday.

Stage Three

Write the subheading: How to get there
Choose from the following:

a) Say how you can get there – by road, rail, sea or air. What roads could you use?

b) Draw a table showing train, coach or plane timetables for a certain day or time of year.

c) Say how you can book a holiday for this place.

d) Draw a map showing how to get there.

Stage Four

Write the subheading: Weather
Choose from the following:

a) Describe the usual weather the place has at different times of the year.

b) Draw a table to show temperature and sunshine for different times of the year or for each month.

c) Say what kinds of things people can do there in good and bad weather.

Stage Five

Write the subheading: The landscape
Choose from the following:

a) Describe what the area looks like – does it have hills, cliffs, farms or hedges, for example?

b) Write about the nice things people can see there as they are travelling around.

c) Write about any kinds of special things there, such as plants, types of farming, animals, birds or buildings.

Stage Six

Write the subheading: Places to visit
Choose from the following:

a) List some of the main villages, towns and cities in the area.

b) Write some information about some of the places to visit. Write about what there is to do and see there.

c) Write about some of the special places to see such as museums, churches or parks.

d) Tell people what different kinds of things there are for adults and children to see and do.

Holiday guide
Vocabulary bank 1

accommodation
amusements

beach
beautiful
bed and breakfast
boat

camping
caravan
cinema
cliff
cottage
countryside

fairground
ferry

guest house

holiday
hotel

motorway
mountainous
museum

path

railway
rain
restaurant
riding
river
road

scenery
self-catering
sport

station
sun bathing
sunny
sunshine
swimming

temperature
theme park
timetable
train
transport
travelling

view

walking
weather
windy

My own words

Holiday guide
Scaffold 2

You are going to write a sporting or activity holiday guide.
To help you write your guide, use the framework below.
Choose one option from each stage, or use your own ideas.

Stage One

Choose ONE sport/activity from the list below.

a) skiing/snowboarding

b) fishing

c) water sports such as water skiing, boating, sailing, diving or surfing

d) horse riding/pony trekking

e) mountain biking

f) hiking

Find out as much information as you can about the activity and the places you can go on holiday to do it.

Use the library, the Internet and CD-Roms to help you.

Write the name of the sporting holiday in big bold lettering as your heading.

Stage Two

Write the subheading: About this sport/activity
Choose from the following to write about:

WHICH SHALL I CHOOSE?

a) Describe the sport and what is involved in doing it.

b) Explain how and why it can be exciting and enjoyable.

c) Explain how and why it is a good idea to go on holiday to do this sport.

d) Describe any special equipment that is used.

e) Explain how the activity is more enjoyable when it is done with other people who are also enthusiastic about it.

Stage Three

Write the subheading: Where to go

Find a map showing where this sport/activity can be done. Either redraw it or cut it out. Give it a bold title and write a caption for it. Then choose from the following:

a) Describe how to get to the holiday area.

b) Describe any interesting things to see on the journey to the holiday area.

c) Add labels to your map to show the location of any interesting things/places.

d) Describe interesting things in the area to see such as birds, animals, good views or buildings.

Stage Four

Write the subheading: Times of year suitable for the activity

Write some paragraphs explaining when is the best time of year to go on this type of holiday in the area you have chosen. Choose from the following to write about:

a) Draw a chart showing the monthly temperatures, hours of sunshine and rainfall for the area. Give the chart a title and label it clearly.

b) Describe the ideal weather needed for the chosen sport/activity and say what time of year it is best to go to the chosen area.

c) Describe the weather visitors would normally expect to find if they go there on holiday.

d) Say what other activities can be done in the area if the weather is not good for the chosen sport/activity.

Stage Five

Write the subheading: Experience, training and qualifications

Find out if it is necessary to have some training or qualifications before going on the holiday. Choose from the following to write about:

a) Describe how to go about getting special training or qualifications to do the sport/activity correctly/safely.

b) Describe what people should do if they have no experience of the sport/activity – are there people who can help on the holiday? Can training be carried out on holiday? Say what it might cost.

c) Say what special insurance is needed, if any, for the holiday.

d) Mention any safety issues that need to be considered.

Remember: use italics or bold lettering to make some words look more important.

Holiday guide
Vocabulary bank 2

accommodation
airport

baggage
boating

canoeing
certificate
challenging
company

dangerous
difficult

entertainment
equipment
experience

fishing
fitness
friends

hiking
holiday

injury
instructor
insurance
interesting

mountaineering

rafting
rainfall
relaxing
risky
rock climbing

safety
sailing
scenery
skating
ski lift
skiing
snowboarding
sunshine
swimming

temperature
thrilling
training
travelling
tuition

views

walking
weather

My own words

How to Make a Paper Aeroplane

The Classic Dart

These instructions are on how to make a paper aeroplane that is designed to fly really well. Changing the design will make it fly in different ways. It is fun to make one that does loops and rolls as it flies. After you have made it, try experimenting with other designs.

Equipment and Materials

You will need: An A4 sheet of paper
You may also need: scissors

What to do

1. First take a rectangular sheet of paper and fold it down the centre dotted line. Open it out again afterwards. (Diagram 1)

2. Now fold the top left and right corners in to meet the centre line. (Diagram 2)

3. Fold the slanting top left- and right-hand edges in once more to lie along the centre line. (Diagram 3a)

4. The result should look like Diagram 3b.

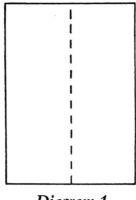

Diagram 1

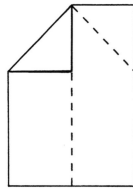

Diagram 2

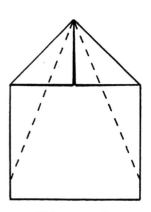

Diagram 3a

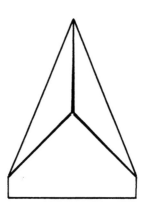

Diagram 3b

5. Now fold the plane in half along the centre line again, making sure it folds inwards. (Diagram 4a)

6. Seen from the side it will look as in Diagram 4b.

7. Fold the long slanting folded edge down to match the lower centre line edge. (Diagram 5a)

8. The result should look like Diagram 5b.

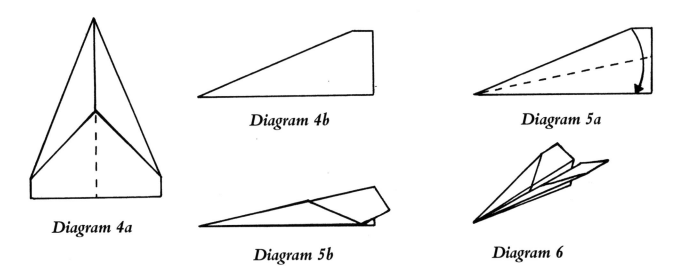

Diagram 4b

Diagram 5a

Diagram 4a

Diagram 5b

Diagram 6

9. Turn over and repeat.

10. Open out the wings to a slight upward angle when looking down the plane from the nose. (Diagram 6)

Flying your plane
Throw slightly pointed upwards. Remember: DO NOT aim at people's eyes and faces – the point of the nose is very sharp!

Try to experiment with cutting flaps in the rear edge of the wings and adjusting them to alter the flight of the plane. You can make a flap by making two short parallel cuts in the rear edge and fold the paper between the cuts up or down.

Watch what happens when you fold the flaps down compared to up.

Watch what happens when you have different flaps on each wing.

For further exciting designs go to: www.paperairplanes.co.uk

How to Row a Boat

Rowing a boat can be very enjoyable. It provides a way of exploring parts of the countryside that can not be reached on foot. The sensation of gliding through the water is very different from walking or cycling. The exercise is also very healthy!

A major difference between rowing and cycling or walking is that when rowing you sit with your back to the direction you are travelling in. This makes it possible to use your weight to pull on the oars. It is important to look round quite often to make sure you know where you are going! Feet should be braced against the back of the boat or against a footstop (ledge) on the floor.

Equipment and clothing

You will need: a boat, oars, lightweight clothing, rubber-soled shoes and a life-jacket.

First attempts at rowing should be done slowly and carefully.

There are four things to do which can be called stages of rowing:
1. Put the oar in the water.
2. Pull the oar through the water.
3. Lift the oar out of the water.
4. Get ready to do the movement again.

1. Put the oar in the water.
◆ The oar should be placed in the rowlock so that it balances well and rests on the water without sinking more than the blade below the water.

◆ Holding the handles of both oars, lean forward so that your nose is over your toes.

◆ Keep your head up. Prepare to put the blade in the water.

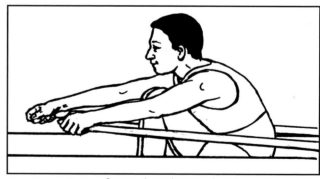

Lean forward with your head up.

2. Pull the oar through the water.

✦ Legs do most of the work at this stage. Push with your feet against the floor or back of the boat. At the same time start pulling with your arms and back.

Pulling the oar provides the power to make the boat move.

✦ Keep your arms straight and swing your back from the hips. Pull the oar handle up to a position just below your chest.

✦ Do not dig the oar too deeply into the water. The blade should be just below the surface.

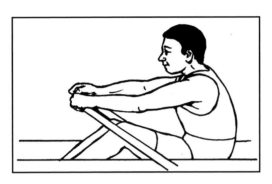

Pull the oar handle to just below the chest.

3. Lift the oar out of the water.

✦ At the end of the rowing stroke your back will be leaning slightly backwards. Take the blade out of the water quickly.

✦ Important: Take the oar out smoothly and **quickly** so that it does not get caught up with the movement of the water. Do this by lowering your whole arm; not just your wrists. If you are too slow and the oar blade gets dragged away, the handle will push against your chest and could knock you to the floor or even overboard into the water! This is called 'catching a crab'.

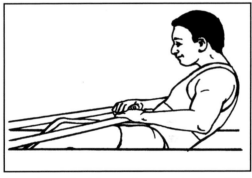

At the end of the stroke your back will be leaning slightly backwards

4. Get ready to do the movement again.

✦ Practice makes perfect. You will probably be rather clumsy at first and things will go wrong. Remind yourself to do each of the four parts of the rowing movement in order and slowly at first. Soon the movements will become regular and routine so you will not have to think about it. The movement will become graceful and smooth. Speed can then be increased but remember to look where you are going!

✦ A sense of achievement can soon be enjoyed as you glide smoothly through the water.

Things not to do Do not leave the oar in the water at the end of a stroke. Do not dig the oar too deeply into the water.	**Things to do** Do look round often to see where you are going. Do start slowly and carefully. Do keep your head up.

Understanding the grammar and punctuation

Verbs

A sentence must have a verb. Sentences cannot make sense without verbs. Verbs are 'doing' words. They are used for actions.

When you write instructions you will use the present tense most of the time. For example:

Holding the handles of both oars, <u>lean</u> forward so that your nose <u>is</u> over your toes.

Instructions use the imperative form of verbs. For example:

<u>Fold</u> the long slanting ...

<u>Turn</u> over and repeat.

<u>Put</u> the oar in the water.

<u>Keep</u> your head up.

Adjectives

Adjectives are describing words.

When you write instructions, adjectives must be used to make the instructions clearer.

Fold the <u>slanting top left-</u> and <u>right-hand</u> edges in

once more to lie along the centre line.

Commas

Commas help the reader to make sense of a sentence or list. They show the reader where to pause for a moment.

A comma is used to separate things in a list.

You will need: a boat, oars, lightweight clothing, rubber-soled shoes and a life-jacket.

Verbs

Draw a circle round each underlined verb that is in the imperative tense.

Lift the boat carefully. It may be heavy.

Rainwater may have collected in the boat. Tip it out.

Launch the boat into the river.

Hold onto the mooring rope!

One oarsman forgot and the boat drifted away!

He swam after it!

Underline the two sentences that should not have been in these instructions because they do not explain how to prepare a boat for rowing.

Adjectives

Fill the blank spaces in the sentences below by using the adjectives in the box.
Use each adjective once only.

gentle, calm, thick, thin, long, wide, cold.

1. *Using _____ paper or _____ cardboard makes the aeroplane stronger.*

2. *Fly the paper aeroplane when there is _____ weather or only _____ winds.*

3. *A _____ narrow rowing boat will go faster than a short _____ boat.*

4. *The water in a river can be deep and _____ so be careful not to fall in.*

On the back of this page, write a set of instructions for making your favourite sandwich. Remember to use adjectives to make the instructions clear.

Commas in lists

Put commas in the correct places in these sentences.

1. *To make a rowing boat you need: sheets of waterproof plywood nails screws glue varnish paint and woodworking tools.*

2. *Good places for flying paper aeroplanes are: school playing fields big gardens playgrounds parks and coastal beaches.*

3. *Paper aeroplanes can be made from thin card copier paper newspaper or sugar paper.*

4. *There are many different types of boats, including: yachts paddle steamers ocean liners barges speed boats canoes fishing boats ferries and dinghies.*

Look at these lists. In each sentence one comma has been placed incorrectly.
Circle the incorrect comma and if you think a comma is missing, write it in.

1. *At Emma's birthday party she received a toy rabbit, a book, two, CDs and a board game.*

2. *My dad has four brothers, three sisters, five uncles, five aunties, four, nephews and two nieces.*

3. *We went to town and we bought a, new sofa some dining chairs and a new table.*

4. *You will need: paper, scissors, glue, paper-clips, ruler, pencil, coloured, pencils and a compass.*

Complete the following sentence, remembering to use commas to separate each item in your list.

If I won £500 I would buy:

Helpful hints for writing instructions

✦ Plan what you are going to write. It is important to get instructions in the right order.

✦ When you have finished planning, use bold headings to make it very clear what it is all about.

✦ You can begin with an introduction. This should include general information that gives some important facts. Try to include some interesting points and even amusing information if you can. This will help to get readers interested. Make it seem enjoyable to do what you will explain.

✦ Instructions can usually be divided up into stages. Organise the information by setting it out with clear headings for each stage. Use subheadings where this helps the reader to find pieces of information. The following should be used for the stages:
  – numbered subheadings with paragraphs
  – subheadings with numbered points
  – subheadings with bullet points.

✦ Words that are sometimes called 'markers' can be used to show there is a logical order. For example, 'Firstly …', 'Secondly …', 'Follow this by …', 'Next, be sure to …' and 'In addition …'

✦ Use the second person when you write. So, do not write using the words 'I', 'me', 'myself', 'mine', 'we', 'us', 'ourselves' or 'our'.

Do use: 'you' and 'your'.

✦ Use clear, simple language. Keep most of your sentences short. Instructions often have to use words that are used in a particular sport or for tools and equipment used. If you have to use words that readers may not know make it clear what the word means with a short explanation.

✦ Include sketches, diagrams or photographs to make parts of the information clear. These must have a title and plenty of clear labels. These labels explain the parts of the drawing or diagram.

✦ Make sure you only write about how to do the activity or make the thing. Do not write about other things.

✦ Make sure you do not repeat things in your instructions. This could cause someone to do something twice!

✦ The length of the information will depend on what you are writing about but try not to make it so long that readers will get bored or confused when reading it. Instructions that are brief and clear are usually best.

✦ When you have finished writing the instructions, write a paragraph to remind the reader of the enjoyment of the activity and suggesting what could be done next to improve on what has been done. A list of things to do and not to do could be included at the end, particularly if there are points about safety to be remembered.

Instructions for making something Scaffold 1

You are going to write instructions about how to make something.
To help you plan how to write it, use the framework below.
Choose one option from each stage.

Stage One

Choose one of the following things.
Be careful to choose one you have made or one you can find information about.

a) kite

b) bird table

c) bird nesting box

d) papier-mâché bowl

e) puppet

f) cake

Write the word for the thing to be made as a heading at the top of your page.
Find out information from books, the Internet and CD-Roms.

Stage Two

Write a list of the equipment, tools and materials needed to make the item.

Put a heading at the top: **Equipment and tools**

Stage Three

Write a paragraph explaining what the instructions are about.
Get the reader's interest by making it seem an enjoyable thing to make and to use.
Choose one of these beginnings:

a) These instructions will tell you …

b) Using this (the thing being made) is great fun …

c) These instructions will help you to try different enjoyable ways of making and using (the thing being made) … including …

Stage Four

Decide the best way to lay out your instructions.
Divide it up into stages.
Choose from the following:

a) numbered subheadings with paragraphs;
b) subheadings with numbered points;
c) subheadings with bullet points.

Use diagrams or sketches to help explain each stage of making the item.

✦ Label the diagrams carefully or number each diagram and write about it.

✦ If it is too difficult to draw the diagram you may be able to photocopy and cut out pictures from a book or use clip art on a computer.

✦ Even if you cannot do a drawing of each stage try to include a picture, sketch or diagram of the finished item.

Stage Five

Write a paragraph at the end to explain how to use the thing that has been made.

Depending on the thing made, there may be a number of ways it can be used.

It might be possible to change it in some way to make it and use it in different ways.

This paragraph should include a reminder of the ways using it can be enjoyed.

You could start this paragraph in one of these ways:

a) Now you have made the _____, using it is even more enjoyable if you remember to …

b) Now you have made the _____, using it is even more enjoyable if you make sure you …

c) Use the _____ by …

Instructions
Vocabulary bank 1

bake	glue	safety
bend		sandpaper
bowl	ingredients	saw
brush		scissors
	kite	screw
cardboard		seed
carefully	make	sew
cook	material	shape
cut	mix	sharp
		slice
drill	nail	sugar
	next	
finally		tools
first	paint	
flour	paper	varnish
fly	plywood	
fold	puppet	water
fruit		

My own words

Instructions for doing an activity
Scaffold 2

You are going to write instructions about how to do an activity such as playing a game or riding a bicycle.

To help you plan how to write it, use the framework.

Choose one option from each stage, or use your own ideas.

Stage One

Choose one of the following activities. Be sure to choose one you have done yourself or one you can find information about.

a) playing a game

b) riding a bicycle

c) canoeing

d) sailing a dinghy

e) playing an instrument

f) using a computer application, such as a simple word processor

Write some words about the activity as a heading at the top of your page.

Remember: write about something you know about and find out extra information from other people who are good at the activity. You should be able to find out more information from books, the Internet and CD-Roms.

Stage Two

Write a list of the equipment and any special clothing/footwear needed.

Put a heading at the top: **Equipment and clothing**

Stage Three

Write a paragraph of introduction explaining what the instructions are about. Get the reader interested by making it seem an enjoyable thing to do. Choose one of these beginnings:

a) These instructions will tell you how to …

b) Learning how to do this is great fun and these instructions will help you …

c) If you are keen to know how to _____ successfully, follow these instructions.

Stage Four

Plan what you will write. It needs to be divided up into stages.
Decide the best way to lay out your instructions.
You could use the following for the stages:

a) numbered subheadings with paragraphs;
b) subheadings with numbered points;
c) subheadings with bullet points.

Depending on the activity you have chosen:
a) Write about where to do it, the cost of doing it and any licences, club memberships or permits needed.
b) Explain the reasons for doing the activity; for example whether it will help to make you fit and strong or make you more skilful.
c) Explain how the activity is organised and any rules for doing it, including safely.

Use diagrams or sketches or photographs to help explain the activity.
Label the diagrams carefully or number each diagram and write about it.
If it is too difficult to draw diagrams you may be able to cut out pictures from a magazine or use clip art from a computer.

Stage Five

Write a paragraph at the end to round off your instructions.

Depending on the activity, there may be a number of ways it can be done.
Explain how it is possible to go on to learn how to get better at doing the activity and to get even more enjoyment from it.

You could start this paragraph in one of these ways:
a) These instructions explain how to get started with (this activity). You can now learn to do it in a more advanced way by ... (For example, going to training sessions, having more practice with people who are good at it, taking part in competitions/contests or watching them.)
b) Now you know how to ... it is even more enjoyable if you remember to... (This paragraph should include a reminder of the ways the activity can be enjoyed.)

Stage Six

An important part of instructions on many activities is safety.

As well as safety advice, include important points from the instructions you have already written.

Write two lists:
A list of things to do. Start each line with the word 'Do'.

A list of things not to do. Start each line with the words 'Do not'.

Instructions
Vocabulary bank 2

activity

backspace
balance
boots
brakes
buoyancy aid
buy

catch/caught
centre
club
computer
copy
court

edit

field

goal
guitar

handlebar
header

jib

keyboard

launching
layout
licence

mast
membership

organisation

paddle
paste
pedals
pedestrians
penalty
piano
point
print
pump

racquet
referee
rules

safety
sail
save
screen
speed

tackle
team/teamwork
text
throw
touch
type

umpire

violin

wheels
whistle
wicket

My own words

Directions to the fairground near Thorpe Park

Directions from the park to the fairground for someone who knows the area

Map 1

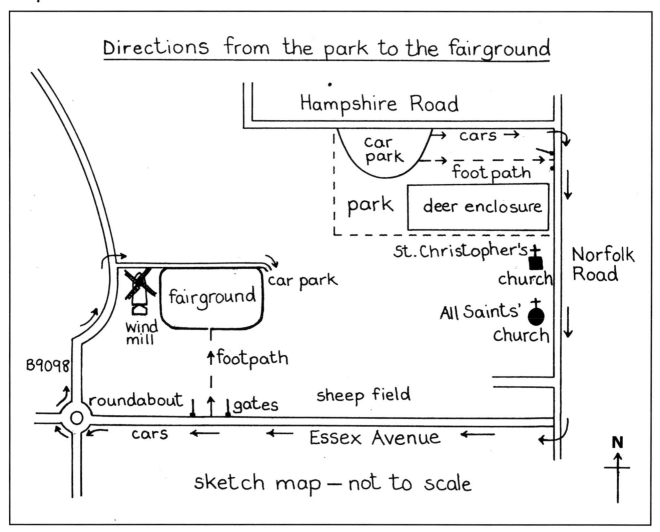

1. Go out of the park through the big gate near the end of the deer enclosure.
2. Turn right.
3. Walk past the two churches and take the second turning on the right.
4. Walk along this road past the field where sheep are sometimes grazing.
5. When you get to a pair of iron gates on the right, go through them on to the footpath.
6. The fairground is at the end of the footpath.

Directions from the park to the fairground for someone who does not know the area.

1. This is a large park and it is very easy to get lost so be careful to walk along the footpath beside the fence round the deer enclosure, until you get to a big gate.

2. Go out of the park through this gate.

3. Turn right and walk along Norfolk Road.

4. 300 metres along Norfolk Road there is St Christopher's Church. Walk past it.

5. Another 200 metres along the road is another church called All Saints' Church. Walk past this church too.

6. Take the SECOND turning on the right, which is Essex Avenue.

7. Walk along this road past the field where sheep are sometimes grazing.

8. Look out for a pair of iron gates at the start of a footpath. Go through these gates onto the footpath.

9. Walk about 100 metres along the footpath and you will see the fairground at the end of this footpath.

Directions for a car driver

1. Drive out of the park's car park and turn right onto Hampshire Road.

2. At the end of the road turn right onto Norfolk Road.

3. A short distance along this road you will pass the park gates on the right and you will see two churches.

4. When you get to the second church, which is All Saints' Church, you will see two right turnings.

5. Turn into the second turning, which is Essex Avenue.

6. Drive along this road past the field where sheep are sometimes grazing.

7. Drive past a pair of iron gates on the right. DO NOT DRIVE THROUGH THEM because this is a footpath and not a road.

8. 200 metres further on there is a roundabout.

9. Take the third exit at the roundabout so you turn right onto the B9098 road.

10. This road curves round to the right and as it becomes straight again there is a windmill on the right.

11. Turn right into the track beside the windmill.

12. 300 metres along the track you turn right into the fairground car park.

Long distance directions

Driving directions from Basingstoke to Thorpe Park theme park

From Basingstoke:

Road	Direction	Details	Distance	Minutes
A30	East	Towards Hook	8 km	10
M3	North east	At Junction 5	23 km	14
M3 onto A322	North	At Junction 3 Past Bagshot	2km	2
A30	North east	Through Sunningdale	8 km	8
B389	East	Past Virginia Water	4 km	4
A320	North east	To THORPE PARK on left	2 km	3
			Total 47 kilometres	Total 41 minutes

Map 2

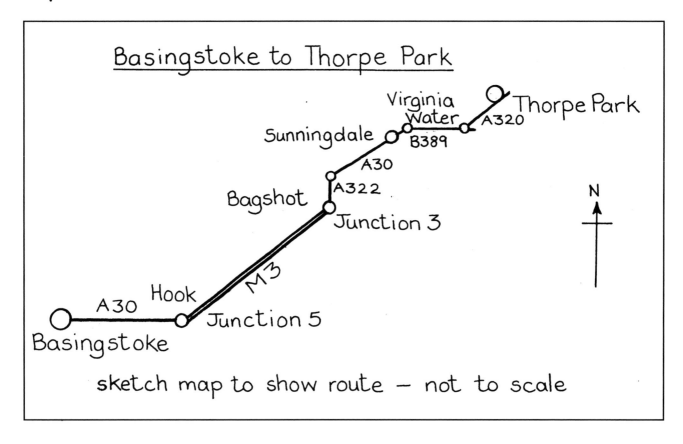

Understanding the grammar and punctuation

Plurals

Plural means more than one.

To make a noun plural, we usually just add an 's'.

One metre   *Two metres*

One gate   *Two gates*

If a noun ends with 's', 'x', 'z', 'sh' or soft sounding 'ch' you add 'es'.

church   *churches*

buzz   *buzzes*

If a noun ends with a consonant then a 'y' you change the 'y' to an 'i' then add 'es'.

baby   *babies*

fly   *flies*

If a noun ends with 'f' or 'fe' you normally change the 'f' or 'fe' to 've' then add 'es'.

calf   *calves*

knife   *knives*

There are some words that do not change at all!

one sheep, two sheep

one deer, two deer

Capital letters

Capital letters are used at the start of every sentence.

Use a capital letter for the first letter of names:

Mr. Samuel Swindler

Monday, Tuesday,

England, Wales, London.

Capital letters can be used to emphasise particular words;

for example, on warning notices.

Take the SECOND turning on the right, which is Essex Avenue.

Plurals

Write the plural form of the noun after each of these singular nouns:

kite _____   enemy _____

cup _____   party _____

church _____   gallery _____

view _____   calf _____

glass _____   knife _____

family _____   hutch _____

Choose a plural noun from the list below to complete each description.

bees, geese, flowers, bells, pigs

A bouquet of _____   A swarm of _____

A gaggle of _____   A peal of _____

A litter of _____

Read these sentences. The words underlined are plurals. Fill in the blanks below so the sentence is changed from plural to singular.

1. The <u>sheep</u> were moved from the farm to the <u>fields</u>.

   The _____ was moved from the farm to the _____.

2. The <u>boys</u> ran over the <u>ditches</u> and along the <u>footpaths</u> to reach the park gate before it was closed.

   The _____ ran over the _____ and along the _____ to reach the park gate before it was closed.

3. Some <u>policemen</u> were standing near the <u>entrances</u> to the fairground.

   A _____ was standing near the _____ to the fairground.

Capital letters

Draw a circle round each capital letter that is wrong in these sentences:

1. In St Christopher's Church There is A big Statue of Jesus Christ.

2. It is Not possible to Take a short cut Along Hampshire Road.

3. When a Boy fell off the Roundabout Dr Leech rushed over to him.

4. At the ENTRANCE to the Fairground, a man was Collecting money for the Royal National Lifeboat Institute.

5. The Book was called, 'Driving Routes in the U.K.'

6. The RSPCA had an Exhibition beside the Entrance to the Car Park.

7. MPs meet in the Houses of Parliament to have Discussions and Debates.

8. The Sign said: 'DANGER. THIN ICE', but the Boy still Walked onto the Lake in the park.

Write each of these sentences in the space provided, using capital letters where you think they should go.

there is a big sign on the gate to the field of sheep: 'important. shut the gate.'

_____

in the fairground there were rides called: 'david's dodgems', 'helen's helter skelter' and 'roger's roundabout.'

_____

_____

the fair, which is one of the largest in Britain, was opened by dr sawbones who arrived in his old mg car.

_____

_____

Helpful hints for writing directions

✦ Plan what you are going to write. Get the directions in the right order otherwise people could get lost!

✦ When you have finished planning, use bold headings to make it very clear what it is all about.

✦ You need to know the route well to give directions accurately. Unless you often travel it, you need to walk or travel along it with an adult. Make notes about directions as you go. Look for buildings and other things that people will recognise. These are called landmarks.

✦ A map or sketch map diagram makes directions much clearer. Most directions can be shown on it. Look at maps of your area. Draw a rough copy of your map first and mark the main places on it. If this is too difficult, you could trace or photocopy a map and use it as a base map to write on.

✦ Read through the notes you made and look at your map. Show the route on the map with small arrows on the map and label the map with places and landmarks along the way.

✦ Draw a final copy of your map. Write a clear heading above it. Put an arrow on the map to show the direction of North. Write the scale or 'sketch map, not to scale'. Draw any signs and symbols you have used and explain what they mean (map key).

✦ It is usually best to write directions as if they are for someone who does not know the area. Think what it would be like if you were going there

for the first time. It is important to give plenty of detail.

✦ When you are writing the directions keep looking at the map and adding notes and labels to it. Think where there are things that are easy to see, such as churches, bus stops, large houses and petrol stations. Describe these landmarks so that people will recognise them and know which way to go.

✦ For someone driving, directions are best shown in a chart or table in quite large lettering. This chart can have columns for the number or name of the road, the compass direction of travel and description details with landmarks. It is very helpful if there are numbers of kilometres or miles for distance and the expected time it will take.

✦ Words that are sometimes called 'markers' can be used to show there is a logical order. For example, 'Firstly', 'Secondly', 'Follow this by', 'Next, be sure to' and 'In addition'.

✦ Do not use the first person when you write. This means, do not write using the words 'I', 'me', 'myself', 'mine', 'we', 'us', 'ourselves' or 'our'.

✦ Make sure you only write about how to get to a place. Do not write about other things.

✦ Make sure you do not repeat things in your directions.

✦ Put the map and the writing together so you have directions that people can follow without getting lost!

Directions
Scaffold 1

You are going to write some directions to a place.
To help you write the directions, use the framework below.
Choose one option from each stage.

Stage One

Choose one of the following:

a) Directions from my classroom to a nearby park/church/sports ground.

b) Directions for a treasure hunt.

c) Directions for people to my home for a birthday party.

Choose to write the type of directions that you already know something about.

Use the words in a), b) or c) as your heading at the top of your page.

WHICH SHALL I CHOOSE?

Stage Two

Find out information about the route.

a) Walk with your teacher or other grown-up to the place you have chosen. Make notes about what you see along the way, including street names.

b) Walk round a route for a treasure hunt with an adult. It could be within the school, in the school grounds or in your garden at home. Make notes about the route.

c) With an adult, walk along the best route to your home. Make notes of things along the way.

Stage Three

Draw a map or plan.
Draw a rough copy first and mark the main places on it.

a) Look at a road map that shows your school and the place you are going to.
   This will help you to draw your map. You could photocopy it and use this as your base map.

b) Use a map of the area where the treasure hunt is to happen to help you. If this is too difficult make one up which might look a bit like the area you know.

c) Look at a road map that shows your home and the best way to get to it. This will help you to draw your map. You could photocopy it and use it as a base map.

Stage Four

Read your notes from Stage 2. Look at your map from Stage 3.
Draw the route with small arrows on the map and label the map with places and landmarks along the way.
Draw a final copy of your map.

a) Draw arrows from your classroom, out of the school, through the school grounds, along roads and footpaths to the destination.
b) Draw on your treasure hunt map the places people have to go to. Label them with numbers. Draw arrows between them.
c) Draw arrows to your home along roads and footpaths to the front door of your home.

Stage Five

Write the directions for someone who does not know the area.
This means you need to give plenty of detail.

a) Look at your map and use your notes from Stage 2 to write instructions about where to go.
b) Use your map and notes from when you visited the area to help you write instructions for each stage of the treasure hunt. Some of the directions may be written as simple clues.
c) Look at your map and use your notes from Stage 2 to write instructions about how to get to your house.

Put the map and the writing together. You should now have instructions that people can follow without getting lost!

Directions
Vocabulary bank 1

bus stop	home	right
	house	road
carefully		roundabout
clue	kerb	
		south
driving	landmark	station
	left	straight on
east		street
entrance	mansion	
exit	memorial	telephone kiosk
		travel
factory	north	treasure
farm		
field	playground	west
footpath	post box	
forest	post office	
	progress	
graveyard		

My own words

Directions
Scaffold 2

You are going to write some directions to a place.
To help you write the directions, use the framework below.
Choose one option from each stage as appropriate.

Stage One

Choose one of the following:

a) Directions for a driver who wants to drive from one town to another and who has not done it before.

b) Directions for a circular walking route through the countryside.

c) Directions for a delivery driver who is to deliver a computer from a shop in the nearby town to your school.

Choose to write the type of directions that you already know something about. Write one of the above as a heading at the top of your page.

Stage Two

Find out information about the route.

a) Use a road atlas to choose two towns and find a route between them. Use a route planning CD-Rom or internet service to get an outline of route directions. Make notes about the route.

b) Walk round the route with an adult, not on your own or only with friends. It could be in a country area near the school or in a large park near your home. Make notes about the route.

c) If you know someone who regularly drives along the route, ask them for help with directions. Use a road atlas to find the route. Use a route planning CD-Rom or internet service to get an outline of route directions. Make notes about the route.

Stage Three

Draw a map or plan. Draw a rough copy first and mark the main places on it.

a) Look at a road map that shows the town you have chosen as a starting point and the destination. This will help you to draw your map. If it is complicated it could be photocopied and used as a base map.

b) Use a map of the area where the walk takes place. Draw, trace or photocopy it to use as a base map to draw on. If this is too difficult make one up which might look a bit like the area you know.

c) Look at a road map that shows where your school and the computer shop are. This will help you to draw your map. Work out the best way to drive to the school with a large delivery van. If the map is complicated it could be photocopied and used as a base map to draw on.

Stage Four

Read your notes from Stage 2. Look at your map from Stage 3. Draw the route with small arrows on the map and label the map with places and landmarks along the way. Draw a final copy of your map.

a) Draw arrows from the town where the driver will start to the town that is the destination.

b) Draw on your map the places people will walk to. Label them with numbers. Draw arrows between them.

c) Draw arrows to your school along roads and footpaths to the vehicle entrance of your school.

Stage Five

Write the directions for someone who does not know the area. This means you need to give plenty of detail. Decide whether you are going to write the instructions in sentences or in a chart.

a) Look at your map, remember when you went there yourself and use your notes from Stage 2 to write instructions about where to go.

b) Look at your map and notes from when you visited the area. Use them to help you write instructions for each stage of the walk.

c) Look at your map and use your notes from Stage 2 to write instructions about how to get to your school to deliver the computer.

Put the map and the writing together. You should now have instructions that people can follow without getting lost!

Directions
Vocabulary bank 2

approach

bridleway
bus stop

carefully
clue
cycle track

delivery
driving

exit

factory
footpath
forest

garage
graveyard

keep left sign
kerb

mansion
memorial

narrow
no entry

one way street
opening

parking
pedestrian crossing
petrol station
post box
post office
public House

railway bridge
restricted
right
river
roundabout

school
signpost
station
straight on

telephone kiosk
track
traffic lights
travel

viaduct

yellow lines

My own words

King James I and the Gunpowder Plot

The first Stuart king: King James I

King James was born in 1566 and was a baby when he became king of Scotland. Helpers, called regents, helped him to rule while he was a child.

As a boy, James was often unwell and had a weakness of the legs. Even though it was difficult, he learned to ride a horse and became very good at it. While he was small he had to be tied on to the saddle so he did not fall off.

He was well educated and was particularly interested in religion. When he became a teenager he started making decisions himself and ruling as a real king.

When the English Queen Elizabeth I died in 1603, James became King James I of England as well as King James VI of Scotland. He said the countries must be called Great Britain although many people did not like this. Something many people **did** like was his new version of the Bible which was much easier to understand. It is called 'The King James Version' of the Bible.

While king of Scotland from a baby, James was nearly 37 when he became king of England. He had pale blue eyes, an untidy thin brown beard, brown hair and thin legs. He was not very tall and looked fat because his clothes were bulky. There was a lot of material in his clothes to try to protect him against being stabbed by daggers if he was attacked.

James's tongue was too big for his mouth. This made it difficult for him to drink and the drink spilled out of his mouth making a mess. He never washed his hands; he just rubbed them on a cloth.

The Gunpowder Plot – 5th November 1605

Many people who were Catholics hated King James because he preferred the Protestant religion (The Church of England). Nowadays, we can pray to any god and be in any religion but 400 years ago people were told by the king or queen that they must pray in the way set out by the Church of England. James was the leader of the Church of England and he punished people who wanted to be Catholics.

Some Catholics were so angry that they got together and decided to kill him. Robert Catesby was their leader. Guy Fawkes was a Catholic soldier who knew how to use gunpowder. They decided to blow up the Houses of Parliament when the king was there. Barrels of gunpowder were secretly put into a cellar under the Houses of Parliament. They then waited for King James I to arrive. Guy Fawkes was to be the one to set light to the gunpowder – but it all went wrong.

Someone found out about the plot. A letter was sent to Lord Monteagle warning him not to go to the Houses of Parliament. He showed the letter to the king. Soldiers were sent to search the cellars. They discovered Guy Fawkes with matches ready to light the gunpowder. He was arrested and put in prison in the Tower of London. The other plotters rushed away on horseback but were caught and shot by the king's soldiers.

Guy Fawkes was later tortured and executed.

The people who liked James celebrated the failure of the Gunpowder Plot by making a dummy that looked like Guy Fawkes and burning it on a huge bonfire. Since then, every year on November 5th, there have been celebrations with bonfires and fireworks.

Notes on this information
James I
Born 1566 & King of Scotland as baby
Poor health but good horse rider & studied religion
1603 also became king of Eng 37 yrs old
J: new Bible version
Thin beard, blue eyes, thin legs
Looked fat because clothes too big for him
Tongue too big so messy drinker

Gunpowder Plot
J punished Catholics so they hated him
Some plotted to kill J
Nov. 5th 1605 Robert Catesby & Guy Fawkes put gunpowder under parliament
J found out
Soldiers caught GF
GF executed; other plotters shot
Bonfire celebrations still happen every 5th Nov

Spider Diagram of Notes on King James I

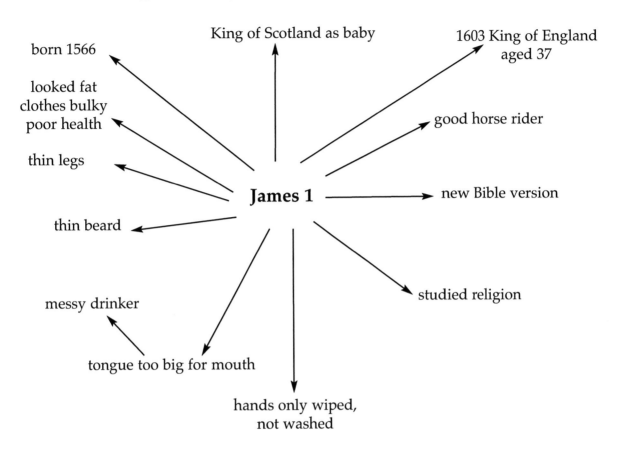

King of Scotland as baby

1603 King of England aged 37

born 1566

looked fat
clothes bulky
poor health

thin legs

good horse rider

James 1 → new Bible version

thin beard

studied religion

messy drinker

tongue too big for mouth

hands only wiped,
not washed

Flow diagram of notes on the Gunpowder Plot

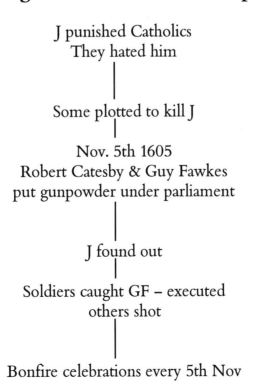

J punished Catholics
They hated him

Some plotted to kill J

Nov. 5th 1605
Robert Catesby & Guy Fawkes
put gunpowder under parliament

J found out

Soldiers caught GF – executed
others shot

Bonfire celebrations every 5th Nov

Understanding the grammar and punctuation

Making notes
Removing words from a sentence and keeping its meaning

Some words can be taken away from a sentence to make it shorter.

Others must be kept so it makes sense.

Removing words is what you do when you make notes.

For example:

James was the leader of the Church of England and he punished people who wanted to be Catholics.

could become:

James punished Catholics.

Commas

Commas help the reader to make sense of a sentence or list.

Commas show the reader where to pause for a moment. They break up the sentence and make it easier to understand. For example:

Helpers, called regents, helped him to rule while he was a child.

A comma is used to separate things in a list. For example:

thin beard, blue eyes, thin legs

Don't use a comma unless it helps the reader to understand the sentence.

Removing words from a sentence and keeping its meaning

In the sentences below, the most important words have been printed in **bold**.
On the lines below, write only the main words.

Guy Fawkes was fighting as a soldier in the Spanish army when the plot was planned by
Robert Catesby. Guy was brought back to England to help because he was a gunpowder
expert.

_____

_____

Now do the same with these sentences. Cross out words that are not important and decide which
words to keep.

1. *The soldiers were searching for gunpowder when they found Guy Fawkes there.*

   _____

2. *Guy Fawkes was caught in the cellars of the Houses of Parliament and was tortured and*
   executed.

   _____

3. *Many people think that Guy was burned at the stake but this was the punishment for a*
   crime against the Church. Guy was hanged and his body was cut up. Hanging was the
   punishment for a crime against the king.

   _____

   _____

Read the notes below. They are about firework displays. Use them to write the information in full
sentences on the back of this sheet.

   5 Nov failure gunpowder plot celebrated – fireworks used
   dangerous in garden – safer go to display
   bonfire barbecue – hot dogs potatoes
   dress warmly – weather cold

Commas

Put commas into the sentences below.

1. Put three commas in this sentence.

   For a firework display to be successful it is best to have plenty of space shelter from the wind a good supply of firewood and lots of different fireworks.

2. Put four commas in this sentence.

   In the town of Lewes in Sussex there is a very big celebration every year on 5th November with a procession a huge bonfire and lots of fireworks.

Rewrite these sentences, putting a capital letter at the beginning, a full stop at the end and commas where you think they should go.

1. *fireworks particularly loud ones can scare pets and other animals*

   _____

   _____

2. *it is best to shut cats and dogs indoors where they can not see the fireworks*

   _____

   _____

3. *the Catholic soldier Guy Fawkes who was probably an explosives expert was chosen to help in the plot to blow up Parliament*

   _____

   _____

On the back of this sheet, write lists to complete the following sentences.
Don't forget the commas!

1. *For my next birthday I would like ...*   2. *My six favourite animals are ...*

3. *Five famous people I would like to meet are ...*

Helpful hints for taking notes

◆ When you are collecting information from books, magazines and newspapers for a project, you need to collect information briefly and quickly. To do this you take notes. Your notes remind you of things you need to write about later.

◆ Notes are often intended only for the person writing them but they can be a short way of giving information to other people.

◆ Notes should be brief but easy to understand.

◆ Notes should be arranged in order.

◆ First look through the pages of a book to get an idea of what you will be making notes about.

◆ If there are headings in the book use them as titles for each part of your notes.

◆ You could also try reading the first one or two sentences of each paragraph to find bits of information to note.

◆ Look at your notes as you go along and cross out any that are not important.

◆ Write only the main points.

◆ If you have a photocopy or computer printout of the pages of information, underline or highlight the main important words of each sentence. Then write just the underlined words in your notes.

◆ Write notes using abbreviations and make up some of your own short words or abbreviations.

◆ Leave out details, descriptions and long explanations.

◆ Descriptions and explanations of what happens can be made into lists.

◆ A diagram can be used to show brief notes and how they fit together.

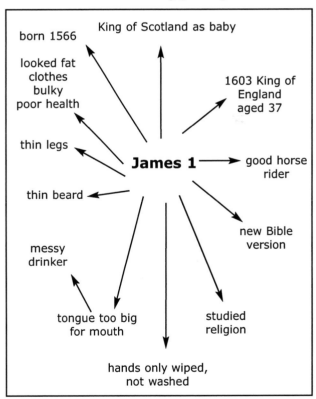

◆ Notes can also be written in columns or on a chart.

Taking notes
Scaffold 1

You are going to take some notes to help you make a spider diagram.
To help you make your notes, use the framework below.
Choose one option from each stage.

Stage One

Choose one of the following kings of Britain.

a) Henry VIII
b) Alfred the Great

Read as much as you can about this person.

Stage Two

Write some sentences about his childhood/early life.
Choose some of the following:

a) Date and place of birth.

b) What his family was like.

c) Things he did when growing up.

d) What he was like as a child.

e) Anything interesting or unusual about his childhood.

Read through your work. Underline or highlight any key words/dates.

Stage Three

Write some sentences about his life as a king.
Choose some of the following:

a) Date he came to the throne and anything interesting about him becoming king.

b) Special things he did as king.

c) Special dates and events during his reign.

d) What the people thought of him.

Continued on next sheet.

Continued from previous sheet.

e) What he looked like, what he liked to do.

f) Who he was married to/names of any children.

g) Date of death – why and how he died.

Read through your work. Underline or highlight any key words/dates.

Stage Four

Choose one special event that happened during his reign. Write some sentences about it. Choose some of the following:

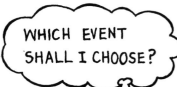

a) The date of the event and why it was special.

b) What happened?

c) How did the people respond?

d) How did the King respond?

e) How/why is this event still remembered today?

Read through your work. Underline or highlight any key words/dates.

Stage Five

Use your underlined words/dates to make a spider diagram about this King. Include the following:

a) Date of birth.

b) Date he came to the throne.

c) Date of death.

d) Any special dates/events during his reign.

e) Special things about him, such as what he looked like, how he behaved.

f) Name(s) of wife/wives and children.

Taking notes
Vocabulary bank 1

Some abbreviations to use in making notes

about . . . . c (circa)
and . . . . +
are . . . . r
as soon as possible . . . . . . asap
be . . . . b
century C
doing . . . . doN
etcetera . . . . etc
example . . . . e.g.
for 4
good . . . . gd
government . . . . gvt
including . . . . inc
London . . . . LDN
Member of Parliament . . . MP
road . . . . Rd
see c
street . . . . St
that is . . . . i.e. (il est)
to 2
United Kingdom . . . . UK
very v
year . . . . Yr
you . . . . u

Now make up some of your own abbreviations and put them in the box below.

Other words for Scaffold 1

appearance
battle
beard
behaviour
brutal
cannon
castle
Catholic
conflict
coronation
events
executed
habits
hair
hanged
heir
marriage
married
persecuted
Pope
praised
Protestant
ruled
ruthless
soldiers
succession
throne
wives

My own abbreviations

My own words

Taking notes
Scaffold 2

You are going to take some notes to help you make a spider diagram.
To help you make your notes, use the framework below.
Choose one option from each stage or use your own ideas.

Stage One

Choose one of the following famous people.

a) Anne Frank

b) Winston Churchill

c) Boudicca

Read as much as you can about his person. Use information books, the Internet and CD–Roms to help you.

Stage Two

Write some information about his/her childhood/early life.
Choose from the following.

a) Details about his/her date and place of birth.

b) Information about his/her family and what they were like.

c) Information about his/her school life, early home life, friends.

WHICH SHALL I WRITE ABOUT?

d) Information about his/her personality, things he/she liked to do.

e) Information about any special events that happened to him/her as a child.

Read through your work. Underline or highlight any key words/phrases/dates.

Stage Three

Write some information about his/her life as an adult. Choose from the following.

WHAT DO I KNOW?

a) Details of any special dates/events in his/her life.

b) Information about his/her marriage/children.

c) Information about what he/she looked like; what he/she liked to do.

d) Date and circumstances of his/her death.

Read through your work. Underline any key words/phrases/dates.

Stage Four

Write some information about why this person became famous. Choose from the following:

a) Detailed information/dates about a special event that helped to make this person famous. What happened? How did it affect him/her?

b) Details of this person's ambitions and how he/she achieved them.

c) What people thought about him/her when he/she was alive and what people think about him/her today.

d) Information about any special awards/medals received and why.

e) Details about how this person's life has had an impact on others.

f) Your opinions about this person.

Read through your work. Underline any key words/phrases/dates.

Stage Five

Use your underlined words to make a spider diagram about this person. Include the following.

HAVE I GOT ALL THE INFORMATION?

a) Date of birth.

b) Marriage details.

c) Dates of any special events.

d) Special characteristics – appearance, behaviour, hobbies/interests.

e) Date of death.

Taking notes
Vocabulary bank 2

Some abbreviations to use in making notes

about	c (circa)
and	+
are	r
as soon as possible	asap
be	b
century	C
doing	doN
etcetera	etc
example	e.g.
for	4
good	gd
government	gvt
including	inc
London	LDN
Member of Parliament	MP
road	Rd
see	c
street	St
that is	i.e. (il est)
to	2
United Kingdom	UK
very	v
year	Yr
you	u

Now make up some of your own abbreviations and put them in the box below.

Other words for Scaffold 2

air force	impressive
appearance	intelligent
army	kind
battle	leadership
beard	marriage
behaviour	married
brick laying	morale-
brutal	boosting
chariot	navy
cigar	patience
clever	persecuted
conflict	praised
courage	prime
defiance	minister
determined	ruled
elegant	ruthless
encouraging	shrewd
events	smoking
executed	soldiers
fearful	speeches
fierce	succession
government	suit
habits	temper
hair	throne
heir	warfare
helmet	wife
horses	

My own abbreviations

My own words

A letter to a friend

246 Stickleback Walk
Smallstream
SS98 7AZ

17/8/03

Dear Praful

We've just got back from a really good holiday.

I wanted to go to another country for a holiday but Dad said we can't afford that until next year. Now I'm glad we stayed in England and went to the Norfolk Broads. I thought it would be boring living on a boat for two weeks. Who would want to do that for a holiday? As it turned out, it was great fun.

Our car broke down on the way there. The AA man had to tow us to a garage at Wroxham. Then we had to carry all our luggage half a mile to the boatyard. Mum was quite cross and tired when we got there so Paul and I kept quiet. Dad, as usual, was quite cheerful. He said we would have a good time and the car would be repaired in time to go home.

The boat looked small but when we got inside it there was quite a lot of room – except Dad banged his head on the roof and said some naughty words! I rushed into the boat and got the best cabin. Paul didn't like that and hit me. You know what he's like. He's about as annoying as a brother can be at times.

The man from the boatyard showed us how to steer the boat. I was on top of the cabin and only just got down in time to go under a bridge! I thought, 'At least I hadn't fallen in on the first day.'

When we set off there were lots of boats on the river. Some of the people on them seemed very happy and couldn't steer straight. One boat went into the bank and got jammed in the branches of a tree.

We went to a big lake called a 'broad'. It seemed a good idea to moor beside the reeds. I jumped off the boat with the mooring rope. I thought I was going to land on hard ground. But guess what? It was mud! I sank in the mud up to my knees. Mum had to reverse the boat to pull me out of the sticky, black, smelly stuff. I slid into the water on the end of the rope and pulled myself up onto the boat. I *had* fallen in on the first day! It's a good thing there was a shower on the boat so I could clean the mud off myself. But the mud blocked the drain hole and Dad had to unblock it!

After Mum had calmed down, things went quite well for several days. We had lots of sunny weather. We had a rowing boat we towed behind. At one place where we moored, we took the rowing boat out to row to a village. The village church had a tower we could go up. We climbed up a long, dark, winding, spiral stairway. Paul kept clapping his hands loudly to hear the echo. He got told off by the vicar! At the top I felt excited and scared at the same time. We could see a long way, right to the distant horizon, but there was a sheer drop right in front of us! The people below looked like ants. I wanted to throw a paper aeroplane over the side but Dad stopped me. He said it would annoy the vicar again and make litter. I sometimes think Dad wants to stop me having fun because his dad stopped him doing fun things when he was a boy. Is your dad like that?

When we got back to the rowing dinghy, Paul stepped on its side and it tipped up suddenly. He went head first into the water, scaring the ducks. This was really funny but it also meant we had to go straight back to the boat with my drippy brother instead of having an ice cream.

The next day it rained and was very windy. Some children on another boat asked us to go onto their boat and do some fishing. I caught a fish called a pike, which had lots of sharp teeth in its big mouth. I wanted to keep it to cook for a meal but the girl on the other boat said that's cruel. I said it's a cruel fish because it eats other fish and it tried to bite me. She grabbed it and threw it back. So I pushed her in after it.

The next day was boring because I had to stay in my cabin all day as a punishment.

When Mum and Dad had calmed down things improved, the weather got sunny again and we went a long way on the boat to visit interesting places. Mum and Dad even let me steer the boat. Have you ever steered a boat? It is exciting and strange. The boat turns a long time after you turn the wheel. Not like a car. It took some time to get used to it. I missed hitting the bridge though and other boats were quite good at getting out of my way.

Dad managed to avoid mooring at big towns because he said it would be busy and noisy to stay near a town. I think it was because he didn't want Mum to disappear all day in the shops.

In the last few days we set off back towards the boatyard. We made friends with a family on another boat going in the same direction. They were in a big old sailing boat, which also had a motor. I went on their boat for a day. Using the sails was great fun. When the wind was strong the boat leaned right over and we went faster than the motorboats. That family got on well with my mum and dad and they invited us to go on their boat with them for a weekend in September. Would you like to come too?

When we got back to the boatyard our car had been repaired so we were able to go home in it. Mum had taken a while to get used to the boat but she ended up enjoying the holiday even more than Dad. She is very keen for us to buy our own boat if we can ever afford it. Can you imagine it? Going out in a boat whenever we want to. Fantastic! Perhaps we won't go abroad next year so we can afford to buy our own boat on the Norfolk Broads.

I'm looking forward to seeing you to tell you lots more.

See you soon,

Helen

PS. If we buy a boat you could come out on it with us. HP

Understanding the grammar and punctuation

Pronouns

Pronouns are words used instead of nouns.

They may refer to things: *it, this, that, those.*

But the mud blocked the drain hole and Dad had to unblock <u>it</u>.

'It' is used instead of repeating 'drain hole'.

Personal pronouns are used for people: *you, I, me, myself, who.*

<u>I</u> had fallen in on the first day!

Possessive pronouns show ownership: *my, mine, yours, hers.*

Other boats were quite good at getting out of <u>my</u> way.

Pronouns are used to show if someone is male or female: *she, he, her, him* and so on.

Punctuation in letter writing

Punctuation in the main part of the letter is done the same way as in any type of writing.

Punctuation in the address and date at the top of a letter can be left out.

246 Stickleback Walk
Smallstream
SS98 7AZ

17th August 2003

You do not need to use a comma after the person's name at the beginning of the letter or after signing off the letter.

Dear Mary

All good wishes
Sue

Pronouns

Write pronouns instead of the words which are underlined. Use pronouns from the list. Rewrite each sentence.

he, it, its, his, her, hers, she

1. Helen grabbed the rope and tied <u>the rope</u> to a post on the riverbank.

   _____

2. The tide comes into the river and causes <u>the river's</u> water level to rise.

   _____

3. Paul jumped on to the bank and <u>Paul</u> slid three metres in the mud before <u>Paul</u> sat down suddenly and tore <u>Paul's</u> trousers.

   _____

   _____

<u>Underline</u> the **personal pronouns** and (circle) the **possessive pronouns** in these sentences:

1. I picked up my camera and took it to him.

2. He took photos of your boat.

3. She told me the boat hook is yours.

4. They took my camera.

Decide which words in the following sentences need changing to pronouns. On the back of this sheet, rewrite them.

1. Helen wanted Helen's friend to come with Helen on Helen's next boat trip.

2. Paul's dad said Paul could steer the boat until Paul got tired.

Punctuating letters

Punctuate this short letter by putting in commas, full stops and capital letters.

947 river walk
bankside
norfolk
NN97 0XX

4th september 2003

dear tom

i went to the river wensum with my friend ahmed on tuesday

we took binoculars so we could see all the different birds flying nesting and feeding in the reeds trees and fields we hid in tom's old wooden boat so the birds couldn't see us

i want to go there again soon would you like to come with me?
please reply as soon as you can

best wishes

andrew

ps have you got binoculars you can bring with you?

In the boxes below write an email from Tom in answer to Andrew's letter. Include commas, full stops and capital letters.

Write an email address in the box at the top to: andrew08@aol.com.
Write a title in the subject box.
Write the letter in the big box.

To:

Subject:

Helpful hints for writing informal letters

Writing letters to friends and relatives can be fun. It is good to receive replies to letters through the post. Here are some ways you can make your letters interesting for people to read.

♦ Make sure you set out the letter properly. Put your own address in the top right-hand corner. Put the date under the address.

Dear ... should be on the next line up against the left margin.

♦ Your letter should start on the next line. The first part of the letter should make it clear what it will be about. Write in a friendly way.

♦ Plan what you will say in your letter. Don't just write what you think of as you think of it. You will probably write about things in the order that they happened.

♦ Put plenty of detail and description in your letter. This should be interesting for the reader. Some funny stories and jokes can go in the letter to make it fun to read.

♦ Write as if you are chatting to the person. Put some questions in the letter. You should get a reply to the questions.

♦ When you write to friends it is all right to use shortened words such as *I've* instead of *I have* and *won't* instead of *will not*. Some words can be ones you only use to friends. These are often called slang.

♦ Just writing about what you ate for dinner or what you watched on television can be boring. Try to write more about unusual and funny things that have happened. You could start a sentence *'It seems amazing but...'* and then write about something that happened that would surprise the reader.

♦ The last part of your letter should talk briefly about the main things you have already mentioned and what you wrote about at the beginning. You could also mention something about what you will be doing soon.

♦ Finish your letter in a friendly way with a comment like *'give my love to...'* and *'don't forget to write back to me'*.

♦ Sign off with *'Love'* for a member of your family or close friend and *'Best wishes'* or *'Regards'* for others. You only need to write your first name because the person knows who you are.

♦ Planning the letter to include everything is best but, if you have forgotten something, a sentence can be added at the end called a postscript. Write *'P.S.'* and then the sentence.

email letters

♦ It is not always necessary to write a complete letter. Shorter notes and messages can be written.

♦ Put the email address at the top and a subject in the subject line. Do not use capital letters for complete words as this is 'shouting'. The email can begin with *'Hello'* or something similar. Do not put your postal address in the email. The computer usually puts in your email address and the date automatically so you do not need to write them.

Informal letter
Scaffold 1

You are going to write a letter.

To help you write your letter, use the framework below.

Choose one option from each stage.

Be sure to set out your letter correctly. Put your address in the top right–hand corner with the date beneath. On the left–hand side of the page write 'Dear.....'

Stage One

You are writing to someone to thank them for giving you a present. Decide who you want to write to.

The type of person will affect the way you write the letter and the words you use.

a) A favourite aunt.

b) A friend you have known for a long time.

c) A teenage cousin who lives in Australia.

Stage Two

Give the reason for writing.

You are writing to thank your aunt / friend / cousin for the present and to say how you are using / enjoying it. The present was:

a) a bicycle;

b) computer equipment;

c) equipment for a sport or hobby.

Stage Three

Explain the present was just what you wanted. Give details.

a) What you like about the present.

b) What your friends think of it.

c) What your family thinks of it.

Stage Four

Tell a story, perhaps with some funny comments, about how you learned to use the present.

a) How you have used it.

b) Where you have used it.

c) When you have used it.

Stage Five

Give some more interesting information about you and the present.

a) How it goes with other things you have.

b) How you can use it to do something you could not do before.

c) Explain (imaginary) photos enclosed that show you using it.

Stage Six

Sign off in a suitable way.

a) Look forward to seeing you sometime soon.

b) With love from.

c) Choose your own type of ending.

And then sign your name.

Informal letter
Vocabulary bank 1

camera
colour
connected
crash
cricket bat
cycling

digital

entertaining
exciting

fantastic
fishing tackle
football boots
friend

gift
great

handlebar

installed
interesting
Internet
I've always wanted

keyboard

manual
monitor

pedals
photograph
printing

racquet
really
remarkable
road

software
speed
steering wheel

terrific
thank you

useful

webcam
wet suit
wheel
wobble
wonderful

My own words

Informal letter
Scaffold 2

You are going to write a letter.

To help you write your letter, use the framework below.

Choose one option from each stage.

Be sure to set out your letter correctly. Put your address in the top right-hand corner with the date beneath. On the left-hand side of the page write 'Dear.....'

Stage One

You are writing to someone to ask them if they would like to come to your school to go to an event. Decide who you want to write to.

The type of person will affect the way you write the letter and the words you use.

a) A favourite aunt.

b) A friend you have known for a long time.

c) A teenage cousin who lives in Australia but is visiting the UK for a holiday.

Stage Two

Give the reason for writing.

Decide what type of event it is to be and explain it.

a) A school play you are in or helping with.

b) A school sports day where you will be taking part in events.

c) A school open day where you will be responsible for an exhibition.

Stage Three

Explain what you and your guest will be doing on the day.

a) You will be taking part and they will be watching.

b) You will be in charge of important aspects and they will be able to see what you are doing.

c) You will want them to help with or take part in what is happening.

Stage Four

Tell an interesting story about a previous event of the same type.

This story will be about what happened: what went well and what went wrong. You could include some amusing things that happened.

a) Everything went well until it rained hard and the school got flooded.

b) Some teachers or pupils did not arrive and your parents had to get involved unexpectedly.

c) When everyone arrived they found the school had no electricity because of a power cut so the event had to take place with battery power.

Stage Five

Sum up the letter.

a) You are looking forward to your aunt/ friend/cousin coming to the school and you hope the event will go more smoothly this time!

b) The last time someone visited the school for an event they got involved in it unexpectedly so it would be best to be prepared for the unexpected.

c) You suggest suitable clothing to wear and things to bring in case anything unexpected happens.

Stage Six

Sign off in a suitable way.

a) Hope to see you soon.

b) With love from.

c) Choose your own type of ending.

And then sign your name.

Informal letter
Vocabulary bank 2

accident
amusing
announcer
attend
audience

barbeque
believe
bric-a-brac
bunting

caretaker
cheerful
competition
corridor
costumes

damage
decoration
display

electricity
entertaining

event
excellent
exciting
exhibition

fund raising

governors

I can't wait

lights
loudspeakers

marquee
microphone

noticeboard

once a year

parents
people

performance
please say you'll come
prizes

raffle tickets
refreshments

special
spectator
stalls
supervise

technology
tombola

unexpected

visitors
volunteer

you'll be amazed

My own words

A letter to inform

246 Stickleback Walk
Smallstream
SS98 7AZ

20th August 2003

The Managing Director
Holiday Boats
River Terrace
Wroxham
NN98 00H

Dear Sir or Madam

I am writing to say how very pleased we were with the boat we hired from you for our holiday on the Norfolk Broads, which commenced 3rd August 2003 for two weeks.

We were particularly pleased with the attitude of your friendly and helpful staff. They were very keen to ensure we understood all aspects concerning the use of the boat.

The boat was in very good condition and very clean. All the equipment was in good working order and no faults developed despite the fact that our lively children made full use of all the facilities. We had a most enjoyable holiday and definitely intend to return for more boating activities in the future.

Please pass on my comments to your staff and convey our thanks and appreciation to them.

I hope this letter will encourage everyone concerned to keep up the high standards of service you so efficiently provide.

Yours faithfully

I Crawler

I. Crawler

A letter to request information

879 Patriot's Crescent
Hometown
Lancashire
HH5 9NW

3rd February 2004

The Manager
The Tourist Information Office
The Harbour
Kingsbridge
Devon
KK7 3SW

Dear Sir or Madam

We always prefer to take our holidays in England. I am writing to ask for information about your area of South Devon.

I am particularly interested in the cheaper bed and breakfast accommodation in your area. If possible, please send me addresses of farmhouses that have this type of accommodation.

We have three children who enjoy spending time on the coast. It would, therefore, be particularly interesting to receive information about beaches within easy reach. I would also like to organise some pony trekking or horse riding for my family. Please supply details of any such opportunities.

The ideal situation would be a farm near the coast, with accommodation and horse riding available. We will be particularly delighted if you are able to find us such an opportunity.

General information about the South Hams area of Devon would be most welcome, plus details of other sources of information we may find in our local library.

I look forward to receiving your reply.

Yours faithfully

Z. Mhetubou

A letter to persuade

708 Manyhouses Terrace
Crampton
Wiltshire
SS9 6WW

10th May 2003

Mr G Funmaker
Parks and Gardens Department
The Council Offices
Circle Square
Boarham
Wiltshire
BB1 9WW

Dear Mr Funmaker

Improvements to the local playground

The parents of Crampton greatly appreciate the fact that you have responded to previous requests for a playground for our children. I am now writing to ask you to consider the installation of more equipment in the playground.

The playground has made a big difference to the opportunities for children to enjoy themselves in this overcrowded area of housing. It is good that they now have somewhere to play football without the dangers of doing so in the streets. However, some more equipment is needed because not every child wants to play football.

The two swings are better than nothing but most playgrounds have a roundabout, a slide and climbing frames. On behalf of the parents and children of Crampton, I am asking you to investigate the possibility of obtaining such equipment to bring the playground up to the standard of most others. It would also be much safer if a soft surface were to be installed.

I know the children would find these extra facilities very enjoyable and I hope these suggestions will be acted upon in the near future.

I look forward to receiving a positive reply.

Yours sincerely

J. Pushy

J. Pushy
Chairman, Crampton Residents' Association.

Understanding the grammar and punctuation

Formal language

Formal language is the type of language used in formal letters.

It is always polite and correct. For example:

The parents of Crampton greatly appreciate the fact that you have responded to previous requests for a playground for our children.

Not: 'Thanks for the playground. The mums, dads and kids like it.'

Slang words such as 'kids' are never used in formal letters.

Nouns, pronouns and verbs

A noun is a naming word; for example, 'house', 'girl'.

A pronoun is used instead of a noun; for example, 'it', 'we', 'he', 'you'.

A verb is a doing word; for example, 'go', 'run'.

A <u>pronoun</u> and <u>*verb*</u> must go together properly.

For example,

<u>We *were*</u> going out.   **Not:** <u>We *was*</u> going out.

<u>I *am going*</u> out.   **Not:** <u>I *is going*</u> out.

Paragraphs

Paragraphs are groups of sentences.

The sentences in the paragraph are about one main thing.

Paragraphs are separated by leaving a line in between them.

Formal language

Underline the **formal** sentence in each of these pairs of sentences from letters.

1. I am writing to express my gratitude for the information you sent me.

   Thanks very much for the info.

2. We apologise for sending you the letter in error.

   Sorry we sent you the letter by mistake.

3. Love and best wishes   Yours faithfully

   from Dave   D. Yates

4. I trust you will give this matter urgent attention.

   Please deal with this a.s.a.p.

Nouns, pronouns and verbs

Rewrite these sentences with the right type of verb to go with the pronoun. The first one has been done for you.

1. I were going to play football.

   I was going to play football.

2. We am going to the new playground.

   _____

3. It were very sunny when we was on the boat.

   _____

4. You is the only person to write and I are sending you the information.

   _____

5. It don't work do it?

   _____

Write the correct type of verb – *is was are* – in each space in these sentences.

1. She _____ going to have a holiday in Devon last year.

2. This year we _____ all going there together.

3. It _____ not in the cupboard or anywhere else I have looked.

4. Ahmed and you _____ going home now.

5. You _____ to collect some letters from the office.

Punctuating formal letters

Read the letter below. It contains no punctuation or paragraphs.
Put in all the missing capital letters, commas and fullstops.
Then draw a black vertical line where you think each paragraph should start.

1067 roach road
broadside
norfolk
BB2 12HK

20th June 2002

the manager
roddfish limited
norwich
NN12 4LN

dear sir or madam

i am writing to express my dissatisfaction with a badly made fishing rod i recently purchased from your company the first time i used it two rod rings broke off i am surprised that the quality of your fishing rods is now so poor my friend has been using your rods for many years and he has not experienced any problems he said your rods are excellent and advised me to buy one this is why i chose your rod your advertising slogan is 'roddfish rods are the best' i can not agree i think this is misleading and dishonest i feel you should check all your rods and make sure they are made to the high standard achieved in the past i am returning my rod for replacement or repair i trust this matter will receive your most prompt attention

yours faithfully

james keenfisher

On the back of this sheet, write a reply to James Keenfisher, pretending that you are the manager of Roddfish Limited. What would you say to him?

Helpful hints for writing formal letters

A formal letter is very different from one you would write to friends. Think of how you would write to a friend. Now think how you would write to your head teacher. There is a big difference. A formal letter needs to be carefully set out and everything needs to be explained clearly and politely. Plan what you are going to say.

✦ Make sure you set out the letter properly. Put your own address in the top right-hand corner.

✦ Leave a line. Put the date under the address.

✦ Leave a line. On the left-hand side, write the address of the person who will get the letter.

✦ Leave a line. Begin 'Dear (Name)' or 'Dear Sir', 'Dear Madam' or 'Dear Sir or Madam' if you do not know their name.

✦ Leave a line. Start your letter. The first paragraph should explain clearly and briefly why you are writing. Use formal words; not friendly words or slang.

✦ In the next few paragraphs write what you want to say. Explain things in detail. Do not use shortened words like 'I'm'. Use 'I am' instead.

✦ Near the end of the letter explain politely and clearly what you would like to be done.

✦ If you have put the person's name at the beginning of the letter, finish with 'Yours sincerely'. If not, finish with 'Yours faithfully'.

✦ Sign your name and then write it clearly below your signature.

Formal messages by email

✦ It is not always necessary to write a complete letter. The most common form of message is now the email sent via the Internet.

✦ Do not put your postal address in the email. The computer usually puts in your email address and the date so you do not need to write them.

✦ Put the email address at the top and be sure to put a subject in the subject line. Do not use capital letters for complete words as this is 'shouting'. The email can begin with 'Dear (Name)' or 'Dear Sir', 'Dear Madam' or 'Dear Sir or Madam' if you do not know their name.

✦ When you email the person the next time you can start with 'Hello' or 'Good morning' and their name.

✦ Formal email messages must be brief so they can be read quickly.

✦ Messages by email go backwards and forwards quickly so once you have contacted a person, replies may be short notes, which are less formal.

Formal letter
Scaffold 1

You are going to write a formal letter.
To help you plan your letter, use the framework below.
Choose one option from each stage.

Stage One

You are going to write to a holiday company to explain that you had a very good holiday with them. Choose from:

a) a package holiday company;

b) an outdoor activity centre;

c) a skiing holiday company.

Write your own address on the top right-hand side of your paper. Put the date below the address.

Make up an address for the manager of the holiday company and write it on the next line, on the left-hand side.

Stage Two

Start your letter with 'Dear Sir or Madam' and write your opening paragraph. State clearly the reason for writing.

a) Explain that you had a very enjoyable and well-organised holiday.

b) Explain that you enjoyed the best holiday you have ever had.

c) Explain that the holiday was much more enjoyable than you thought it was going to be.

Stage Three

Use the next paragraph to give more detail.

a) State where the holiday took place and the date you departed.

b) State which holiday centre you visited and when.

c) State that you knew little about the place where you went for the holiday and were delighted when you arrived on (give date).

Stage Four

Use the next paragraphs to describe the
holiday and what you really enjoyed about it.
You may choose more than one of these
options to write about.

a) The staff were very helpful and friendly. Explain why and how.

b) The accommodation and equipment were very suitable, clean and comfortable. Describe and explain fully.

c) You enjoyed the activities and excursions to various places. Describe and explain them.

d) The location of the holiday was very suitable and made it possible for you to get to things you enjoy quickly and easily. Explain how this helped you enjoy the holiday.

e) The very large amount of equipment and activities included in the holiday were a pleasant surprise and very enjoyable. Explain fully how you enjoyed them.

Stage Five

Sum up the message of your letter.

a) You were sad when the very enjoyable holiday ended and look forward to your next holiday.

b) You learned how to do new leisure activities. You will be using these new skills, which will remind you of the good times you had on holiday.

c) You will remember all the very enjoyable parts of the holiday and think of them often during the coming year until you can visit again.

Stage Six

Close your letter

HOW SHALL
I FINISH
THE LETTER?

a) I had a most enjoyable holiday and definitely intend to return for more holidays in the future.

b) Please pass on my comments to your staff and convey my thanks and appreciation to them.

c) I hope this letter will encourage everyone concerned to keep up the high standards of the holiday facilities we enjoyed.

Finish the letter with 'Yours faithfully'.
Sign your letter and write your name clearly beneath your signature.

Formal letter
Vocabulary bank 1

appreciate

beautifully decorated
benefit

circumstances
cleanliness
comfortable
communication
company
considerable
convenient
correspondence

enjoyed
enjoyment
entertaining
excellent views

favourable

holiday

I look forward to
I would be grateful if
in addition
inform
initially

on behalf of

pleased
praise
prompt attention

regarding
responsible

satisfied
suitable

thank you
the highest possible
   standard
tidy

variety

with reference to
wonderful

My own words

Formal letter
Scaffold 2

You are going to write a formal letter.
To help you plan your letter, use the framework below.
Choose one option from each stage.

Stage One

You are going to write to an organisation to do one of the following:

a) To inform (give information)

b) To request information

c) To ask for improvements

Set out the headings for your letter in the correct way.

1) Write your own address.

2) Date your letter.

3) Address your letter to the manager of the company. Make up an address.

Stage Two

Start your letter with 'Dear Sir or Madam'.
Choose one of these organisations to write to.

a) A holiday organisation

b) A sports and leisure centre

c) A supermarket

Stage Three

Write your opening paragraph. State clearly the reason for writing.

a) You like the service provided so far.

b) You are interested in what the organisation does and want information for a school project.

c) You are suggesting what could be done to improve the services and facilities.

Stage Four

Use the next paragraph to give details.

a) Explain what you particularly like about the organisation, its services and facilities.

b) Explain how you have used their facilities for several years and are interested in knowing more about any future additions and improvements planned.

c) Explain that some aspects of the organisation's facilities are boring and not good enough. Suggest how improvements could be made.

Stage Five

Add more details to develop your comments fully.

a) Ask the manager to pass on your comments to the staff and say how pleased you are with their efforts.

b) Ask where you might be able to get more information about the type of organisation from any other sources.

c) Ask if there will be improvements like you suggest in the future.

Stage Six

Sum up your letter and sign off correctly

a) You hope your comments will encourage staff to keep up the high standards.

b) You would be grateful for a reply and information soon.

c) You hope your suggestions are helpful.

Sign off with 'Yours faithfully' and write your name clearly below your signature.

Formal letters
Vocabulary bank 2

adequate
appreciate
assistance
assure
attitude

beautifully decorated
benefit

changing facilities
check-out
circumstances
cleanliness
comfortable
communication
considerable
convenient
correspondence

enjoyment

entertaining
excellent

facilities
favourable

helpful

I look forward to
I would be grateful if
in addition
inadequate
inform
initially
investigate

on behalf of

pleased
products

prompt attention

regarding
responsible

satisfied
special offers
suitable

the highest possible
        standard
tidy
trolleys

variety

with reference to
wonderful

My own words

The Bleatbrook Chronicle

LIFEBOAT GOAT RESCUE

A herd of goats faced drowning when the River Chelwater burst its banks.

GOATS TRAPPED BY FLOOD WATER

The River Chelwater reached its highest ever level and suddenly broke through flood defences early on Saturday morning. A small herd of goats were tethered in their shed at Buttfight Farm, near Bleatbrook. The water surged around their shed and trapped them. As the water rose, they had to stand with front hooves high up on the shed wall to keep their heads above water. The rope tethers stopped them from escaping.

ANIMALS PANIC

Loud panic-stricken bleating woke the farmer and his wife, Arthur (59) and Andrea Landworker (58). They rushed into the field and were immediately up to their waists in water. Unable to reach the goat shed, they could hear the awful sounds of their distressed animals trapped in the shed.

They hurried back to telephone for help. The local policeman reported an RNLI inshore lifeboat had come up river from the harbour and had rescued some people from flooded houses. An emergency radio call was made to the lifeboat crew.

RNLI MAN USES AXE

In the early light of dawn the lifeboat sped up the river to the flooded farm. The water was deep enough for the lifeboat to go straight to the goat shed. Lifeboatman Greg Bravemariner said afterwards, 'We could hear the bleating as the goats desperately tried to keep their heads above the rising water level but we could not open the shed door. I broke down the door with an axe. I tied a knife to a pole and used it to cut the tethers holding the goats down. They immediately swam past the boat but went the wrong way – towards the river!'

SWIMMING GOATS ROUNDED UP BY LIFEBOAT

Lifeboat coxswain Andy Navigator explained, 'I had to steer the boat carefully round the swimming herd and turn them towards dry land. They quickly rushed up onto the next field – on to dry land. Mr. Landworker took the goats into a barn where a heater dried and warmed the shivering animals.'

Mr Landworker said, 'This came as a big shock. The river has not flooded for twenty years – not since the high bank was built to stop the floods. We are very pleased the lifeboat was nearby. This must be one of the most unusual rescues in the history of the lifeboat service! We will be moving the goat shed well away from the river flood plain.'

The Hopscotch News

HOUSES IN FLOODED AREAS MAY BE ABANDONED

Flooding now far more frequent

Angry homeowners demand more protection

The far more frequent flooding by the country's rivers has caused affected residents to demand more to be done to protect their homes from being swamped – sometimes several times a year. The alarming response from the Rivers Agency was that some often-flooded houses should be knocked down and the unfortunate residents rehoused away from the river.

Residents are being told to move away from this flood-prone area.

Home polluted by sewage

Mr. Duckfoot, 51, geography teacher, of Riverside Estate, Deepford, Yorkshire, said, 'The Earth's atmosphere is getting warmer. This causes more water to be evaporated, which, in turn, makes more rainfall. No one seems to understand the river is receiving more water from extra rainfall and it is running off into the river much more quickly from all the new buildings and roads. This causes the river to flood my home with smelly, muddy water polluted with sewage.'

Flooding should be expected

The Rivers Agency has claimed everything possible has been done to stop flooding. Hundreds of millions of pounds have been spent building embankments and new drainage channels. Mr. Buckpass, 48, Rivers Agency spokesman insisted, 'If people choose to live on the flood plains beside rivers they should expect flooding to affect them.'

He asked, 'Is it right for the majority of house owners to have to pay for more and more improvements and repairs through taxes and insurance premiums, to protect a small number of homes that should not have been built near rivers?' Buckpass went on to claim, 'House building companies should not build near rivers. If they do, they should pay for flood protection.'

House builders may pay

The argument is about money for flood protection. Discussions are to take place next month, between the Rivers Agency and the house building companies, to move the families worst affected by flooding and to find the money to protect other houses more effectively.

Understanding the grammar and punctuation

Adjectives

Adjectives are **describing** words. In newspaper reports they are used to make the information more interesting and to get attention.

'This causes the river to flood my home with smelly, muddy water polluted with sewage.'

Verbs

Verbs are doing words.

'I had to steer the boat carefully round the swimming herd and turn them towards dry land. They quickly rushed up onto the next field - on to dry land.'

Every sentence must have a verb because it shows the action taking place. Newspaper reports are full of things happening.

The **past tense** is used for most parts of newspaper reports because they mainly explain what *has* happened.

'I tied a knife to a pole and used it to cut the tethers holding the goats down.'

Dialogue punctuation

Quotation marks (speech marks) are used to show the actual words spoken by people.

Mr. Buckpass, 48, Rivers Agency spokesman insisted, 'If people choose to live on the flood plains beside rivers they should expect flooding to affect them.'

A comma or a colon is put just before the start of the quote.

Adjectives

Fill the blank spaces in the sentences below by using the adjectives in the box.
Use each adjective once only.

muddy	loud	heavy	deep	dark	angry

1. The _____ river was full of _____ water.

2. The _____ sky threatened to cause more _____ rain.

3. _____ people whose houses were flooded near the river made _____ shouts of protest outside the Rivers Agency offices.

Put the opposite adjective from the list in the following sentences.

shallow	clean	light

1. Dirty water stains carpets when it floods a house.

    _____ water stains carpets when it floods a house.

2. Heavy rain caused the river to flood.

    _____ rain caused the river to flood.

3. The deep water made it possible for the lifeboat to reach the goat shed.

    The _____ water made it possible for the lifeboat to reach the goat shed.

Explain what is wrong with these sentences now you have changed the adjectives?

_____

The past tense of verbs

Match the present tense to the past tense of each of these verbs.

Present tense	Past tense
rescue	ran
bleat	swam
run	rescued
think	bleated
swim	thought

Dialogue punctuation

Put speech marks around the words actually spoken in these sentences.

1. *The wildlife warden said, The swans like to swim in the flooded fields to find worms and other food.*

2. *A mother shouted to her child: Come away from the riverbank. The deep water is dangerous!*

3. *Catch the mooring rope! yelled a man as he rapidly passed on his boat, adrift in the strong current.*

4. *Mr. Landworker explained: Our goats are kept for milking. Some people prefer goat's milk to cow's milk.*

5. *Who will pay for better flood defences? asked Mr. Duckfoot.*

Ways of presenting texts

Look at some magazines and newspapers. Look at all the many different types and sizes of print. In this box, write some examples of the ways the writing can be made more interesting and easier to read.

In this box, draw an example of how speech is often shown in a cartoon or comic strip.

On another sheet of paper, draw (or cut out and stick) a picture from a newspaper or magazine and write a caption (a sentence below it, explaining what it shows).

Helpful hints for writing a newspaper report

Newspaper reports are written to tell the reader what has happened. Newspapers want to get attention so they sell as many copies as possible.

Structure

✦ Write a headline that stands out and gets attention. Use big, bold letters, for example the bold fonts on a computer word processor.

✦ Write your first paragraph to tell your reader the main, most important things. Imagine the reader will ask questions about what happened, starting with the words 'who', 'what', 'where', 'why', 'when' and 'how', so you should include the answers to the questions.

✦ In the second paragraph write the details of the story. Think carefully about the details and people you write about.

✦ When you mention people write the name, age and occupation of that person. You could say where they live.

Mr. Duckfoot, 51, geography teacher, of Riverside Estate, Deepford, Yorkshire.

✦ In some more paragraphs write the other information and people's comments, using speech marks. Put the information in the right order so it makes sense.

✦ In the last paragraph say what will happen next.

Discussions are to take place next month, between the Rivers Agency and the house building companies.

Layout

✦ Using a computer and word-processing or desktop publishing programme can be an interesting way to make your writing look like a newspaper. Lay out the newspaper report in a way that makes it easy to read with:

> headlines;
> subheadings;
> columns;
> pictures;
> captions.

✦ There are some words that show the order that things happen in. Some words help people read through the writing easily. Try to use some of these words:

after, meanwhile, then, from where, despite, according to police..., it is believed...

Style

✦ Write in a way that is easy to read. Give information in a few words in mainly short sentences, especially in the first paragraph.

✦ Many different ages and types of people read the newspaper reports, so make sure what you write is clear and easy to understand.

✦ Remember to use speech marks for things that people have said.

Newspaper report
Scaffold 1

You are going to write a newspaper report. To help you plan your report, use the framework below. Choose one option from each stage. Read through each stage carefully and then plan your page layout.

Stage One

Imagine you are writing for a local paper called 'The Informer'.
You are going to write a report on one of the following.
You will need to give your readers all the facts.

a) A ship is wrecked on the coast in a severe storm.

b) A forest fire happens during a drought.

c) An earthquake destroys a city.

Choose one of the following headlines.

a) Disaster and destruction

b) Many rescued from severe danger

c) Survivors celebrate miracle escape

Or make up one of your own.

Write your headline in big bold letters.

WHICH STORY SHALL I WRITE?

Stage Two

Write a short opening paragraph. Use the following to help you.

a) Describe briefly the main points of what happened.

b) Rescue services were successful and solved many problems to bring people to safety.

c) Many people were affected by the disaster and had to be helped.

Remember to explain when, where and why the disaster happened in writing this paragraph.

Stage Three

In the next paragraph give more details. Choose some of the points below to write about. Put some subheadings in your writing.

a) There is much damage. Describe it.

b) Many people were unhappy at their losses. Explain the problems.

Continued on the next sheet.

Continued from the previous sheet.

c) Some people are very happy because they and their relatives survived. Give details.

d) Rescuers received thanks and praise from people who were saved.

e) Animals that ran away were found and returned to their owners. Write about some of the animals.

f) Some evil criminals took advantage and stole things while police were helping with the emergency. This is called looting. Give details.

g) Soldiers helped to rescue and look after survivors. Explain how.

Stage Four

In the next paragraph give some background information. These ideas will help you to think of things to write about.

a) The disaster happened because people were careless and ignored warnings.

b) This type of disaster has happened several times before.

c) Not enough equipment was available for rescue workers to do their job properly.

Stage Five

People have spoken to you about what happened. Use these ideas to help you write what some people said.

a) Mr. Jones, a man who was badly affected by the disaster: 'It was awful. I have never experienced anything like it before...'

b) Rachel Rosenthal, a girl who was rescued: 'It's amazing. I thought I was going to die...'

c) Gurmeet Patel, a rescue worker: 'It was one of the most difficult rescues I have been involved with. I had to...'

Stage Six

Write your last paragraph explaining what will happen next.

a) The rescue workers will be having a meeting to discuss how another disaster can be prevented or made less serious. Give some details.

b) Plans are being made to repair and replace what has been damaged and destroyed. Give some details.

c) Extra doctors and nurses are travelling to the area to treat people who have been hurt. Explain how they are bringing more equipment and medicines.

Newspaper report
Vocabulary bank 1

accident
alarm
angry
anxious

burning

cargo
collapse
control
crashing

damage
dangerous
destroyed
distress

emergency
explosion

fearful
fierce
first aid
flare

havoc
heat
hospital
hull

improve
injuries

lifeboat

mast
medical

panic

raging
relieved
replaced
retrieved
ruined

scorched
shaking
sightseers
smoke
steam

treatment

victims
volunteers

wrecking

My own words

Newspaper report
Scaffold 2

You are going to write a newspaper report. To help you plan your report, use the framework below. Choose one option from each stage.
Read through each stage carefully and then plan your page layout.

Stage One

Imagine you are writing for a national newspaper: 'The Hopscotch Herald'. You are going to write a report on one of the following. You will need to give your readers all the facts.

WHICH SHALL I CHOOSE?

a) A pollution incident

b) Damage to wildlife habitats

c) Problems with drought in parts of the continent of Africa

Choose one of the following headlines.

a) Disaster threatens people and animals

b) Rush to escape

c) Action needed to stop disaster

Or make up one of your own.

Write your headline in big bold letters.

Stage Two

Write a short opening paragraph. Use the following to help you.

a) Describe briefly the main points of the problems.

b) Give some sensational comments that catch a reader's attention.

c) Write some things that some people might disagree with to get the attention of readers.

Remember to explain briefly what, when, where, why and how the problems affect people and wildlife in writing this paragraph.

Stage Three

In the next paragraph give more details. Choose some of the points below to write about. Put some subheadings in your writing.

a) Much damage and suffering occurred. Describe the scene.

b) Many people are unhappy about what has happened. Explain the problems.

c) Some people are relieved because they and their animals survived. Give details.

e) Animals and birds that were affected have been saved and have been treated and found new homes. Write about some of them.

Stage Four

In the next paragraph give some background information. These ideas will help you to think of things to write about.

a) Some careless or greedy people have ignored warnings and caused the problems. Give details.

b) Changes in weather and/or climate have caused the problems or made them worse.

c) This type of disaster has happened several times before.

d) Not enough has been done to stop this type of disaster happening.

Stage Five

People have spoken to you about what happened. Use these ideas to help you write what some people said.

a) Mr. Jones, a man who was badly affected by the problems: 'It was awful. I have never experienced anything like it before...'

b) Rachel Rosenthal, a girl who is very keen to protect the environment: 'This should never have been allowed to happen. The government should have...'

c) Gurmeet Patel, a worker with the International Environment Protection Agency: 'It was one of the most difficult problems to solve and put right. We had to...'

Stage Six

Write your last paragraph explaining what will happen next.

a) The organisations concerned with these problems will be having a meeting to discuss how another disaster can be prevented or made less serious. Give some details.

b) Plans are being made to replace what has been damaged and badly affected. Give some details.

c) Scientists and other experts are travelling to the affected area to work on the prevention of more problems and damage. Explain what they will try to do.

Newspaper report
Vocabulary bank 2

accident
angry
anxious
atmosphere

collapse
conservation
contaminated
control
crashing

damage
dangerous
desertification
destroyed
devastation
distress
drinking water

effluent

emergency

fearful
fierce
food chain

havoc
heat
hospital

improve
insects

migration

ocean

poisoned
protection

relieved
replaced
reptiles
retrieved
ruined

scorched
sightseers
smoke

thirst
treatment

vegetation
victims
volunteers

wrecking

My own words

Encyclopaedia extract

Chalk

Chalk is a soft white rock. It is a type of limestone that has formed on the bottom of the sea and is made up of millions of shells from tiny dead sea  creatures. The main masses of chalk were formed between 140 and 70 million years ago. Some of this chalk has been pushed up by movements like those that cause earthquakes so that hills are made. Chalk can be seen in the white cliffs at Dover where the hills have been worn away by the waves.

Chalk was used to write on blackboards in classrooms before felt pens and white boards replaced it. Chalk broken up into powder is used in making paper and paint and has been used in powder for cleaning teeth.

Glass

Glass is a hard transparent material which light easily passes through. It does not rot or dissolve so it lasts a long time. Window glass keeps out cold and rain but lets in  light. Bottles and windows are often made of easily made cheaper glass which is fragile and breaks easily. Some types of glass are made very strong by special processes such as adding layers of plastic between layers of glass. Water and other liquids cannot get through it therefore it is a good material for containers like bottles and jars. Glass mirrors reflect light. Glass can be shaped to make lenses that magnify and can be used in spectacles, telescopes and binoculars.

Glass is made out of pure white sand which is melted at a very high temperature. Other materials like powdered limestone are added to the sand to make different types of glass. Glass is recycled by heating broken glass, melting it, then adding it to the melted sand. As it cools it is shaped to become solid glass window panes, drinking glasses, lenses, etc.

Granite

Granite is a very hard igneous rock. It is usually pink or grey and consists of quartz, feldspar and pieces of mica that reflect light like tiny mirrors. Granite was 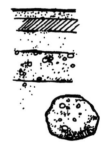 formed ages ago when molten rock called magma slowly cooled below the Earth's surface. Crystals of quartz which look like smoky glass, coloured feldspar crystals and shiny mica formed in the rock because the molten magma cooled slowly.

Because granite is very hard and strong, it is very good for making curbs, paving blocks and statues. It is also good for building large buildings although its hardness makes it difficult to cut granite to the right shape. This makes it expensive to use.

Limestone

Most types of limestone are light grey in colour – almost white in some cases. Carboniferous limestone has cracks and joints in  it that let water into the rock. The water often causes caves and potholes to form in this type of rock. Limestone is formed from sea shells and corals that have been pressed together on the sea floor. Layers of limestone have been pushed up by movements in the Earth's crust to form hills and mountains. This rock is easier to cut to the right sizes and shapes than granite so it is used in buildings. Limestone is dug up in quarries and is used in making cement. Crushed limestone is used for the surface of roads and is put into furnaces with coal and iron ore when making steel.

Rock

The Earth's crust is made of rock. Rocks are mostly solid, hard and heavy. Some are harder than others. Granite is very hard but chalk is soft.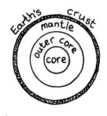
Slate breaks up into waterproof sheets of hard but quite brittle rock.

Rocks are made up of minerals, rather like making a cake. The amounts of mineral ingredients are different for different types of rock. Some rocks have actually been baked by volcanic heat, making them hard like a burnt cake. A rock can be made from the remains of living things. Coal is a rock made from dead plants pressed very hard together. Limestone is made from huge numbers of seashells pressed together. Iron ore is a rock which can be heated to a very high temperature so that liquid iron comes out and can be used to make steel.

Slate

Slate is a hard but quite brittle rock. It is a grey rock which is usually seen as flat sheets used on the roof of a building to keep out the cold and rain. It is a rock  made of very tiny pieces of other rocks that have been worn away into powder. This powdered rock, called clay, has then been pressed together underground. It splits easily into flat, thin, smooth sheets that are waterproof. As well as being used for roof tiles, slate has, in the past been used as a sheet to write on with chalk. Each child in a classroom would have had a slate and a piece of chalk to write on the slate. This was much cheaper than using paper.

Steel

Steel is a silvery, light grey metal – a very hard and very strong material – that is made by humans from rocks.  The rocks used are iron ore, limestone and coal. These are put into a furnace and heated to a very high temperature so that the rocks melt and join together. When the liquid cools it becomes steel.

Steel is used to make a huge number of different things in factories. Some examples are car bodies, knives and forks, the framework of buildings, furniture and washing machines.

Understanding the grammar and punctuation

Joining sentences using conjunctions

Sentences can be joined together using words called conjunctions.

Examples of conjunctions

after, although, as, because, before, if, since, so, that, though, until, unless, when, and, whenever, where, wherever, whereas, while

The following two sentences can be joined by using 'and':

Crushed limestone is used for the surface of roads.

It is put into furnaces with coal and iron ore when making steel.

The result is:

*Crushed limestone is used for the surface of roads **and** is put into furnaces with coal and iron ore when making steel.*

Commas and dashes

A comma (,) or a dash (–) can be used to show a pause in a sentence.

Because granite is very hard and strong, it is very good for making curbs, paving blocks and statues.

Steel is a silvery, light grey metal – a very hard and very strong material that is made by humans from rocks.

Conjunctions

Use a conjunction from the list below to join these sentences:

| after   so   but   because |

1. Chalk lets water soak through it _____ it is called a porous rock.
2. Granite is expensive to use in building _____ it takes a lot of work to shape it.
3. Many people explore caves in limestone _____ it can be difficult in the dark.
4. We will visit the limestone quarry _____ we have had lunch.

These sentences have been joined with the word 'and'. In the space after 'and', write a better conjunction. Then cross out 'and'.

1. Castles have draughty openings for windows and _____ it would have been better if glass could have been used in them.
2. Steel is used to build bridges and _____ it is very strong.
3. Slate can be used for roofing tiles and _____ those made from clay are more common.

Rewrite these three sentence as one sentence using conjunctions to join them.

1. Some types of plastic are transparent. Some types of plastic can be bent. Glass cannot be bent like plastic.

   _____

   _____

2. I will fix the glass into the door. You will hold it steady. You will stop it falling on the floor.

   _____

   _____

Commas

Write commas in these sentences where you think they should go.

1. Although bricks are usually made out of clay they can also be made out of glass.
2. Because granite blocks are heavy it is important not to drop them on your foot!
3. In order to make things from wood you need a saw a drill chisels a plane a screwdriver and screws.
4. When rock is cut from a quarry it can harm the appearance of the countryside.
5. Even though a quarry may not look nice at first it can be made after some time and with much work into a lake for water sports.

Dashes

Rewrite these sentences using dashes where you think they should go.

1. An ideal container for liquids unfortunately rather fragile is the glass bottle.

_____

_____

2. Rocks often contain fossils remains of dead animals and plants trapped between the layers of rock.

_____

_____

3. The container, which cracked, was made of glass something I did not realise at the time.

_____

_____

Helpful hints for writing an encyclopaedia entry

Research

✦ Find information to put in the explanation by reading books, using CD-Roms and the Internet.

✦ Make notes and choose the main points from each piece of information you find.

Planning

✦ Plan what you will write. For each thing you write about include:
  - a description: of appearance
  - structure: what it is made from or what parts of it are like
  - properties: what it can do
  - formation: how it grows, forms or is made; where it comes from
  - use: how it is used, eaten or uses other things.

✦ When you have planned, you will be ready to start writing the information. Use a bold title to make it clear what the information is about.

Writing

✦ When you are writing about a number of things, arrange them in alphabetical order like in a dictionary.

✦ Write the explanation so it is easy to read and understand. Write it in your own words. Don't just copy it all from an encyclopaedia.

✦ If the information for something is quite long, organise it by setting it out with clear headings for each paragraph so that this helps the reader to find pieces of information.

✦ Use clear, simple language. Try not to use words that readers may not know, unless you make it clear what the word means with a short explanation.

✦ Use a mixture of short and long sentences. You can make some longer sentences by using conjunctions.

✦ Include drawings to make parts of the information clear. These must have a caption and, if relevant, plenty of clear labels. These labels explain the parts of the drawing or diagram. Photographs can be included. A computer can be used to place photographs and labels in the right place.

✦ Make sure that what you write is only about what is in the title and headings. Don't write about other things.

✦ Make sure you do not repeat things in your explanation unless it is to emphasise a very important point.

Encyclopaedia entry
Scaffold 1

You are going to write some encyclopaedia entries and put them in alphabetical order.
To help you plan your writing, use the framework below.
Choose one option from each stage.
Read through each stage carefully and then plan what you will write.

Stage One

You are going to write three encyclopaedia entries. Choose one of these types of encyclopaedia so you can write about three animals of one type.

WHICH SHALL I WRITE ABOUT?

a) Encyclopaedia of pets.

b) Encyclopaedia of zoo animals.

c) Encyclopaedia of farm animals.

Write a heading to show the type of encyclopaedia you have chosen.

Stage Two

Think of three animals you will write about.
It helps to choose ones you know something about and ones you can find information about.

You need to write the explanations in your own words. Do not copy out a whole encyclopaedia entry exactly as it is.

a) Three types of pet.

b) Three types of zoo animal.

c) Three types of farm animal.

Write each explanation on a separate piece of paper so they can be arranged in alphabetical order later.

Write a heading for a different animal at the top of each piece of paper.

Stage Three

Start by describing the animal.

Write a paragraph to describe some of these:

a) its coat or skin: fur, scales, wool;

b) the colours of the animal;

c) the size of the animal: about how long and high it is;

d) features of the animal: shape of body and head, length of legs, unusual features;

e) fierce, gentle, friendly, active, fast moving.

WHAT SHALL I WRITE FOR THIS PART?

Stage Four

Make a picture of the animal and label it.

a) Draw a picture of the animal. Write some labels on it to explain the different parts of the animal. Write a caption under it.

b) Cut out a picture from a magazine. Stick it on the paper where you are writing the explanation. Write a caption and labels on it.

c) Photocopy or trace a picture of the animal. Cut out the picture. Stick it on the paper where you are writing the explanation. Write a caption and labels on it.

Stage Five

Write a paragraph about one of these:

a) where the animal lives when it is looked after by people;

b) where the animal lives in the wild and comes from;

c) what type of shelter the animal needs.

WHICH SHALL I CHOOSE?

Stage Six

Write a paragraph about what the animal eats:

a) what other animals it eats;

b) what plants or vegetables it eats;

c) what mixture of foods it prefers.

As you have written about each animal on a separate piece of paper you can now arrange them in alphabetical order like they would be in an encyclopaedia.

Encyclopaedia entry
Vocabulary bank 1

accommodation
agriculture
appearance

barn
basket
bedding
bowl
budgerigar
bull
burrow

cage
coat
coloured

dangerous

elephant

fast moving.
feeding
female
fencing
fierce
friendly
fur

gentle
gerbil
giraffe
grass
grooming

habitat
hamster
hay
horse
housing

insects

meat
milking

paddock
parrot

rabbit

scales
sheep
size
skin
straw

tinned food

wool

My own words

Encyclopaedia entry
Scaffold 2

You are going to write some encyclopaedia entries and put them in alphabetical order. To help you plan your writing, use the framework below. Choose one option from each stage. Read through each stage carefully and then plan what you will write.

Stage One

You are going to write five explanations like the type you find in encyclopaedias. Choose the type of encyclopaedia.

a) Encyclopaedia of building materials
b) Encyclopaedia of cooking ingredients
c) Encyclopaedia of liquids

Write a heading to show the type of encyclopaedia you have chosen.

Stage Two

Think of four materials you will write about. It helps to choose ones you know something about and ones you can find information about.
You need to write the explanations in your own words. Do not copy out a whole encyclopaedia entry exactly as it is.

a) Five types of building materials such as brick, tiles, stone, cement, plastic.
b) Five cooking ingredients such as flour, sugar, salt, pepper, rice.
c) Five liquids such as milk, water, orange juice, oil, petrol.

Write each explanation on a separate piece of paper so they can be arranged in alphabetical order later.

Write a heading for each material at the top of each piece of paper.

Stage Three

Start by describing the material.

Write a paragraph to describe some of these aspects of the material:
a) colour
b) texture
c) appearance
d) taste (if a food or drink)
e) smell
f) other properties of the material: heavy, flexible, solid, strong, brittle and so on.

Stage Four

Draw a picture or diagram to show the material and an example of how it is used. Write some labels on it.

a) Draw a picture or diagram of the material. Write some labels on it to help describe it. Write a caption under it.

b) Cut out a picture from a magazine showing where the material has been used to make something. Stick it on the paper where you are writing the explanation. Write a caption and labels explaining it.

c) Photocopy or trace a picture of the material being used. Cut out the picture. Stick it on the paper where you are writing the explanation. Write a caption and labels on it.

Stage Five

Write a paragraph about one of these:

a) where the material is obtained: from the underground, from rocks, from plants, from the sea, and so on;

b) how the material is obtained: by mining, quarrying, growing, and so on;

c) how the material is processed and prepared for use: by cooking, washing, cutting, heating, refining, and so on.

Stage Six

Write a paragraph explaining the various different ways the material is used.

Write about examples of what can be done with it.

a) What can be made from it.

b) How it makes a difference when used e.g. flavouring, lubrication, washing.

c) How it can be used, consumed and replaced.

As you have written about each material on a separate piece of paper you can now arrange them in alphabetical order like they would be in an encyclopaedia.

Encyclopaedia entry
Vocabulary bank 2

appearance

brick
brittle
building

cement
cleaning
construction
consume
cooking

dense
durable

flavouring
flexible
flour
fluid

fuel

heavy

ingredients

liquids
lubrication

massive
materials

oil
orange juice

pepper
petrol
plastic
potatoes

replaced
rice

solid
spices
stone
sugar

taste
texture
tiles
timber
tomatoes

washing
waterproof
weather resistant

My own words